Relationship Resolution

By Evette Rose

Edition 1

ISBN: 9798875629808

Disclaimer

All information obtained from Evette Rose, or anything written or said by her, is to be taken solely as advisory in nature. Evette Rose and Metaphysical Anatomy™ will not be held personally, legally, or financially liable for any action taken based upon their advice. Evette Rose is not a psychologist or medical professional and is unable to diagnose, prescribe, treat, or cure any ailment. Anyone using the information in this book acknowledges that they have read and understand the details of this disclaimer. Evette can discuss the metaphysical explanations for psychological disorders but are unable to diagnose, prescribe, treat, or claim to cure any illnesses that require medical or psychiatric attention. The principles taught in Metaphysical Anatomy™ and in this book is based on Evette's life experiences and are guidelines and suggestions to support those seeking simple tools to improve their quality of life. By utilizing and using this book, the participant acknowledges that he/she assumes full responsibility for the knowledge gained herein and its application. Material in this book is not intended to replace the advice of a competent healthcare practitioner. The reader takes full responsibility for the way they utilize and exercise the information in this book.

Legal

All recordings and publications obtained from Evette Rose, or this book remain the intellectual property of the aforementioned and must not be used or reprinted in any way without the written permission of Evette Rose. Any unauthorized commercial use of Evette Rose's name, photograph, images, or written material is strictly prohibited and is in direct violation of rights.

ACKNOWLEDGMENTS

Thank you to each and every client or student that I have met for your insight, support, and willingness to share your life stories. I would not have been able to write this book without you! Thank you, Noemi Idang, for your unconditional support!

With Love,
Evette Rose

Also by the author

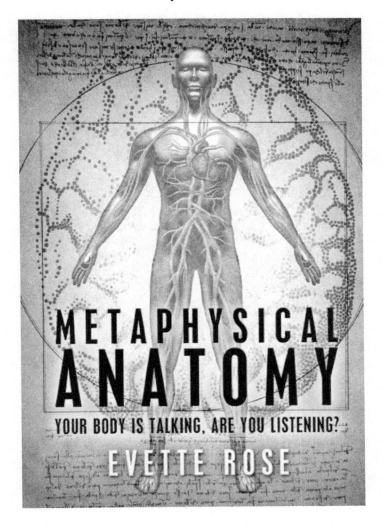

Metaphysical Anatomy is about 679 illnesses from A – Z. This book is so much more than the emotional components of each disease. Metaphysical Anatomy also includes step-by-step guide for identifying the origin of the disease process, whether it be in your ancestry, conception, womb, birth, or childhood. This book is equally valuable for experienced alternative healing practitioners, psychotherapists, hypnotherapists, personal development coaches and those interested in self-healing.

Psychosomatics Of Children
Your Ancestry is talking
Are you Listening?

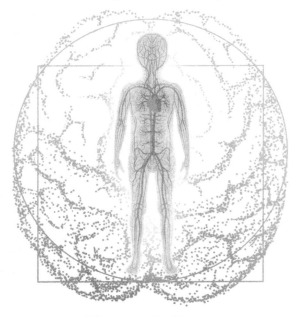

Evette Rose
METAPHYSICAL ANATOMY VOLUME 3

Psychosomatics of children is the sister book of metaphysical anatomy volume one. This book focuses on children's ailments and psychological challenges. Children have not had a full life yet. Therefore, ailments in their bodies are stemming from womb and ancestral trauma, which is unresolved. Not only is your body talking in this book, but your ancestry is talking, are you listening?

DECODING
Trauma

A DIFFERENT PERSPECTIVE ON TRAUMA

Evette Rose

Trauma Decoded. It's time to get back to who you really are! This book is for people who want to change their lives but don't know where to start or what steps to take first, because they have never looked at themselves before, or because they have tried everything else and failed so badly that they feel like a failure and it's easier not to try again than risk failing again, which would make them feel even more of a failure. You are not destined for failure! You are destined for greatness!

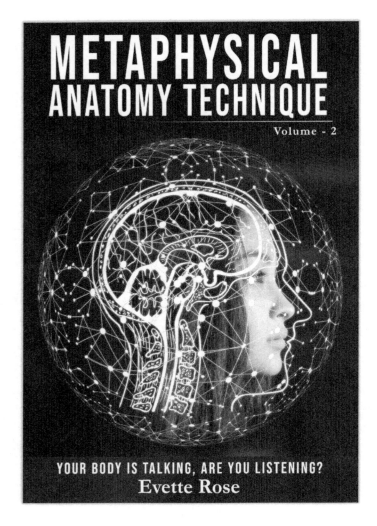

Metaphysical Anatomy Technique Volume 2 explains the core foundation and healing technique behind Metaphysical Anatomy Volume 1 which describes step-by-step guide for identifying the psychosomatic pattern related to 679 medical conditions. These conditions can be activated by circumstances in your present life, your ancestry, conception, womb, birth trauma, childhood, or adult life. Volume 2 teaches you the foundation of Volume 1 including a powerful healing technique. There is also an Online Healing Course that you can combine with Volume 1 and Volume 2.

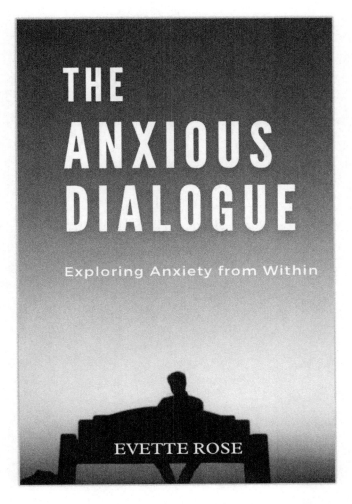

"The Anxious Dialogue" is a self-help book that helps you get unstuck, live with more ease, and feel better. It's a workbook for your mind, heart, and nervous system. It's a quick read with tons of exercises to help you challenge your thinking patterns and change the way you respond to stressors in your life." It has exercises and practical advice that will help you stop your anxiety from controlling your life. You'll learn to identify the patterns and habits that keep your anxiety going, then choose new ways of thinking and behaving to replace them. You'll also be able to practice this new way of being immediately with fun, easy-to-use steps to help you relax and reduce stress.

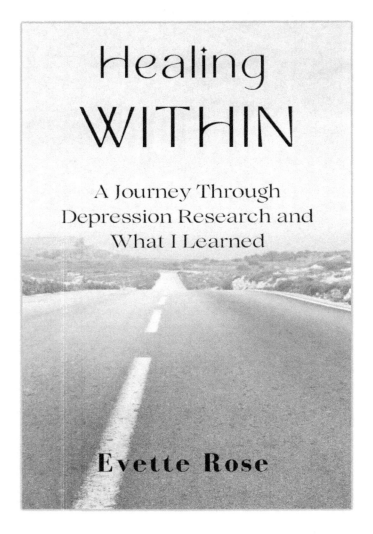

Depression can be a heavy, difficult-to-lift weight. It can sap your energy and make it hard to motivate yourself. But depression is a real condition that often requires treatment. There are many different types of depression, with various causes. Some people experience depression in response to a specific event, while others have ongoing, long-term problems that contribute to their depression. Depression can affect anyone, regardless of age, race, or gender. It's not always easy to recognize, but there are ways to get help.

"The Pain Puzzle" is a book about pain and how to deal with it. Chronic pain affects millions of people worldwide, but there's still so much we don't understand about it. Our goal for this book is to give you the tools you need to understand with your own pain, as well as share some of our findings from research on the topic." If you're suffering from psychosomatic pain, emotional pain, or any other type of ailment pain, "The Pain Puzzle" can help you understand your pain from a new perspective. The Psychosomatics of pain refer to the idea that our thoughts and emotions can contribute to pain. For example, someone who is constantly worrying about their pain may find that their pain gets worse. Our understanding of pain has come a long way, especially in my research. In this book, I will share my research regarding pain, chronic pain, and psychosomatic pain.

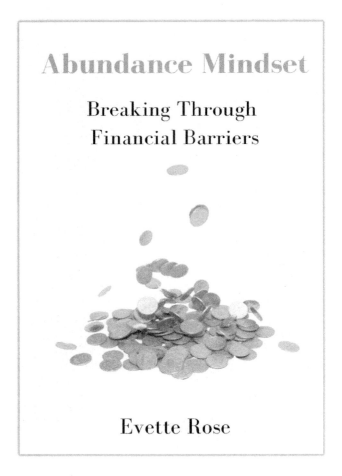

Address your abundance mindset to create prosperity and abundance. Manifest success and heal blocks to abundance with this powerful financial tool. Get clear about your values and ancestry to empower your financial future. Create awareness around your relationship to money for lasting change. This is a great guide to getting your money in order and becoming successful. Get blocks off your energy and start achieving your goals with this helpful guide to financial awareness. Heal your relationship with money and achieve abundance with this valuable guide to financial ancestry. Discover your values and manifest wealth with this enlightening guide to financial success. If you can resolve and release these issues, you will open yourself up to a more prosperous future.

"Boundary Breakthrough" is a self-help book that will help you reclaim your life. It's a guide to understanding and setting healthy boundaries and learning to say no when you need to. If you've ever felt trapped or held back by your relationships, this is the book for you. "It is relatable, and packed with information that will change your life for the better. If you're tired of feeling like you're constantly walking on eggshells, it's time to get your boundaries back! This book will help you set healthy limits and finally start living the life you deserve. build resilience and thrive in the face of adversity, this is the book for you!

"The Content Code" is a life-changing book that will show you how to be happy. It's packed with powerful techniques and strategies that will help you overcome unhappiness and trauma. You'll finally be able to find your purpose in life and achieve your birthright to happiness. This book is engaging, and easy to read - perfect for anyone who wants to start living a happier life today! It's a guide to overcoming trauma and negative associations that hold you back from happiness.

Communication Blocks

A Journey in Understanding Communication

Evette Rose

"Navigating Communication Blocks" is a communication tool designed to help you become more effective and successful at communicating with others. It is based on the premise that most people have some sort of block when it comes to communicating effectively. By becoming aware of these blocks, you can resolve them and improve the way you communicate with other people. This will lead to better relationships, more success in your career, and greater happiness overall.

"Elevate Yourself" is a book that will help you release your past self-sabotaging patterns, clear out your negative associations with yourself, heal your confidence, and more. This book is all about finding love for yourself, no matter what you've been through. It's about learning to forgive yourself for the things that have happened to you in the past or even recently. It's about letting go of old stories that keep you stuck. It's time to shine your light!

"Embrace the Heartbreak" is a guide for turning your life around after a relationship. It includes exercises that will help you discover the root of your problems and give you tools for moving forward with grace and ease. This book is for anyone who has ever questioned their self-worth or felt lost in love. This is a self-help book that helps you heal from heartbreak, divorce, relationship challenges, and abuse. It shows you how to manifest the love of your life and values into your life. This book helps you change the negative patterns in your life, such as sabotage and regret.

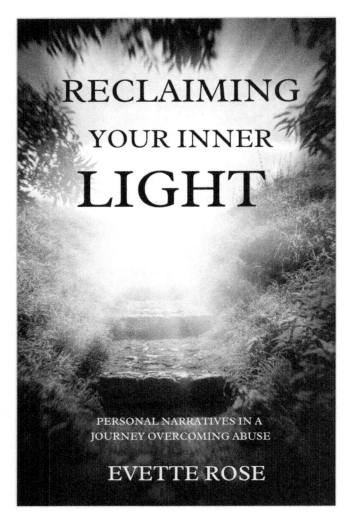

Are you tired of being abused? It's time to break the silence! I can relate because that person used to be me. In this book share my life story, the good the bad and ugly. Being raised in a violent home along with a drug addicted, alcoholic parent trying to navigate my way through what seemed to be the beginning of the end. "Reclaiming Your Inner Light" is here to help you heal from the trauma of abuse and become the confident person you were meant to be.

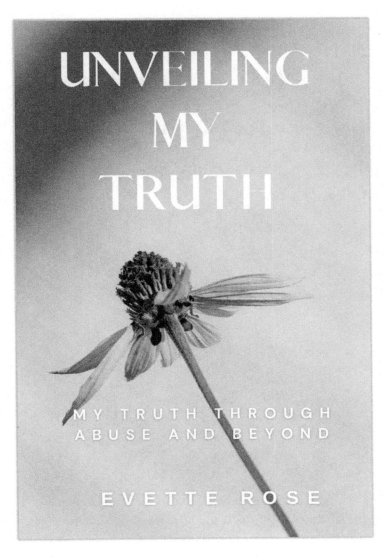

This true-life story is a must-read for people who have either experienced abuse or care about someone else who may be trapped in processing their childhood experiences. This book brings an empowering message of hope, healing and understanding to anyone who feels challenged by their past.

"Relationship Resolution" is a guide to healing relationships, trauma, anger in relationships and gaslighting. If you're dealing with a narcissist or controlling partner, this book has the solutions you need. Figure out your language for love, boundaries, dating, marriage, and more. Learn about the language of love and boundaries so that you can communicate effectively with anyone in your life. "Relationship Resolution" provides tools to help you heal from narcissistic abuse by learning how to recognize gaslighting. This book will also help you understand abuse and control games in your relationships. It will teach you how to set boundaries, communicate effectively, and love yourself.

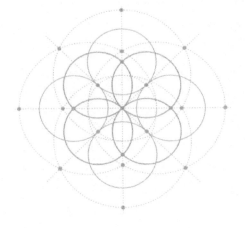

Transform
Everyday

Healing quotes and daily journaling

Evette Rose

The healing intention of this book is to create awareness of your blocks and patterns. It is through awareness that healing, and transformation takes place. In this book you will find quotes and inspirations designed to heal and transform every day of the year.

Table of Contents

Getting started

Hi, my name is Evette Rose and welcome to my world. I look forward to starting this journey with you to dive deep into challenges that you might be having in your life. Congratulations for taking active steps to improve your quality of life it takes courage to make a decision, but it takes determination to follow through on the decision that you made. Know that during this journey you are exactly where you need to be.

I invite you to move through this book with ease and with grace with an open mind.

I would love to stay in touch with you and you can join me on any of my events I always have weekly free master classes and free mini workshops.

You can join me on social media hang out have fun and enjoy a tremendous amount of free content that I also share.

Find me at: www.evetterose.com

Free MAT Membership site: www.matmembers.com

Free Masterclasses: www.matmasterclass.com

Introduction

People form relationships for a variety of reasons, including love, companionship, mutual interests and benefits, reproduction, financial stability, and even to gain social approval. Although relationships may form for many reasons, they all have some level of interdependence between the people involved.

Interdependence can be defined as a mutual or reciprocal dependence of two or more things. In other words, each person in the relationship is dependent on the other for something. This could be emotional support, financial stability, or simply companionship. Each person in the relationship brings something unique to the table and without that contribution, the relationship would not be the same.

One of the most important aspects of any relationship is communication. Communication is how we express our needs and wants to others, and it is also how we receive information from them. It is essential for every couple to have open and honest communication in order to maintain a healthy relationship.

There are many different types of relationships, including romantic relationships, family relationships, friendships, and work relationships. Each type of relationship has its own unique set of challenges and rewards. No matter what type of relationship you have, it is essential to remember that all relationships require effort and commitment from both parties in order to be successful.

Relationships can fail for a variety of reasons, including lack of communication, unrealistic expectations, infidelity, and financial problems. However, the most common reason for relationships failing is that the couple simply stops putting in the effort required to make it work. If you are not willing to work on your relationship, it is likely to fail.

It is important to remember that relationships are not easy, and they require a lot of hard work from both parties involved. If you are not willing to put in the effort, then you should probably consider ending the relationship before it becomes too difficult.

In conclusion, relationships are formed for a variety of reasons, and they all involve some degree of interdependence. Communication is essential for any relationship to be successful. All relationships require effort and commitment from both parties in order to be successful. If you are not willing to work on your relationship, it is likely to fail.

Chapter 1

We want relationships that make us feel happy, loved, and valued. We want to be around people who support our goals and make us better versions of ourselves. We want relationships that are healthy and enriching, where both parties feel good after being around each other.

Healthy relationships should make you feel good about yourself and leave you feeling supported and loved. If a relationship is making you feel bad, or like you're not good enough, it's not a healthy relationship.

In a healthy relationship, both parties should feel happy, supported, and valued. If you don't feel this way, it's time to reassess the relationship.

Do you feel like you can be yourself around your partner? In a healthy relationship, you should feel like you can be yourself without fear of judgment or rejection. You should feel comfortable being honest and open with your partner.

Do you feel like your partner supports your goals and dreams? In a healthy relationship, your partner should be your biggest cheerleader. They should support your dreams, and goals, and help you to achieve them.

Do you feel like your partner makes you a better person? In a healthy relationship, your partner should make you feel like the best version of yourself. They should challenge you to be a better person and help you to grow and develop as a person.

If you can answer yes to these questions, then you are in a healthy relationship! If you answered no to any of these questions, it's time to reassess the relationship. Healthy relationships make us feel good about ourselves and leave us feeling supported and loved. If your relationship isn't making you feel this way, it's time to reconsider whether it's a healthy relationship for you.

Union between partners

A divine union between partners is a spiritual connection that is said to be incredibly powerful and pure. It is said to be so profound that it can bring about feelings of oneness and unity between the two people involved. Some believe that this type of connection is what allows us to experience the highest level of love possible. A connection that allows two people to become one and to share each other's energy and soul.

Divine unions are said to be rare, and many people believe that they are reserved for only the most special relationships. There are those who believe that such a connection can only be made between twin flames - two people who are said to be mirror images of one another, and who share the same soul. Others believe that any two people can form a divine union, provided that they are truly dedicated to one another and have an open and pure heart.

No matter what your beliefs may be, there is no denying that the concept of a divine union is an incredibly beautiful one. In this context I'm also referring to the relationship itself and the emotional and soulful connection that should be present in a healthy relationship. Why is this important? Because at the end of the day, that's what matters. It is like a pole between two people which binds them together.

It is the essence of love, the energy that binds people together. A strong union between two people can withstand life's challenges. The connection stems from the center of each person and connects them in such a way that it creates a mutual understanding, respect, love, and passion for one another.

That bond keeps people together, even in the middle of a storm and even when things are going wrong in their lives. Maybe there are traumatic events, and life itself has become so stressful. But, I mean, look at COVID. How many relationships didn't last because of it? So, this is what I'm referring to. The connection was not strong enough to withstand the storm and what it revealed.

Primarily, we are all compatible when considering our spirituality and the way we operate. There is a beautiful and dynamic connection where there can be a spiritual essence, where a certain platform can be connected and established, where there's an equal foundation of exchange, and just connecting and just being present also matters.

Relationships are about more than just action in bed. We build relationships with our presence, such as being with one another without feeling the need to do something all the time, being together, and enjoying each other's company. When you observe all your relationships, present or past, and think about what they would have been like if you didn't always feel the need to "do" things to make the relationship tick? Constant communication issues, challenges, everything. If you strip it all away, what are you left with? Are your relationships strong? What do you see or feel?

Is there a connection? Is there something pulling you in closer? Or do you feel, "Oh, there used to be a pull, but I forgot because I was so busy "doing" I disconnected my awareness of this connection in the relationship?"

Forced actions can completely ruin a divine flow between two people in a relationship. Even our ancestors experienced what could flow between two people coming together in partnership.

How two people show up in a relationship has changed over time because societal values and our values change and advance.

During our ancestry, men had a specific role, and women did as well. These roles and definitions are changing daily, which gives birth to a new way of entering a relationship, and our subconscious patterns self-sabotage is also moving to new heights.

Looking at the hierarchy of society, we should take out the equation that men are better than women. We have to bring it back to a soul level, especially when looking at native tribes; they showed a tremendous awareness of this. Sometimes these native tribes were far from each other, and couldn't always communicate, or didn't even have time to fight because one of them was always out hunting, fighting wars, working or whatever the reason might be. But that's just how things were back then.

My point? Something keeps people together, whether it's a divine union, a shared magnetic pull, or a soul connection. Sometimes, people get together who are still building their connections. However, they know they are nurturing a powerful potential between them.

Sometimes a union is formed because of an arranged marriage. Often there was an intellectual love at first sight, meaning the connection of the heart wasn't there at first. But maybe you had a fantastic conversation, and you just intellectually connected with this person. Either way, you found commonality, and then the soul connection (union) was established.

A connection can be there from the start or it can grow over time. If your compatibility and the foundation on which you're building this relationship are healthy, you can build a lasting partnership.

So apart from a connection that can help a relationship withstand challenges. Our definition of what a relationship is even more important. Because based on this definition, you will attract a partner who is in alignment with this definition. If you don't have a clear definition, then your dating life might be messy. What is your definition of a relationship? Does your partner or past partners fit that bill?

The way you will ever feel a divine union is if you feel safe with your partner. Sometimes there is a union, there is a beautiful flow, and there is a connection. However, we can't feel it because we're not open to receiving it because of fear. That is what we're going to be looking at now.

So, let's get our writing pads out. Let's define what a divine union is in a relationship. What should it look or feel like? What is your definition?

Divine   union   is   when   people   come   together   and

_____

For example, a definition could be to be together and not always having to do something. What does that look like, sitting on the beach and just watching the sunset, or just sitting in a park and lying on the grass just looking at the clouds? Cook dinner together, only sometimes needing a full-blown conversation. That's what makes a relationship strong, being able to just "be" with each other.

There are a few things that are important in any relationship. You need to be aware of each other's emotional well-being. Trust each other and understand one another. Most importantly, love should not be conditional. You should feel safe and have a sense of freedom. This is a good definition already.

My next question is, what should you be doing that you are not doing when you look at your previous answer? This can help you expand your definition. What is it you're not doing that you probably know you should be?

_____

For example, a partner may have expected too much. This could mean expecting the other partner to invest the same amount of energy into the relationship. Instead, what would have helped was to realize that people have different ways of investing in a relationship. Something might have been meaningful to one partner, but not to the other.

Communication in relationships is also important. I mean, that is a no-brainer. If your communication sucks, then you are most likely destined to fail if you don't correct it.

Another question is, "what's holding you back from creating this divine union?"

_____

It can be anything, a negative thought, an emotion, a pattern, or an incident.

Here is another question: "What is your greatest need in a union?"

_____

So, this is a good start, but what are your greatest needs in a union? For many people, it is to feel safe and knowing that they will not be abandoned. We all need to feel a sense of belonging. My next question is: If you healed this unmet need, would you still feel drawn to your partner?"

_____

Was your union built on fulfilling an unmet need? Keep that in mind. When two people are in a relationship based on their unmet needs, it rarely ends well. They often cannot meet each other's needs, which leads to frustration and resentment. It's often a recipe for disaster.

In the end, you have to decide what you ultimately want in a relationship. If this feels challenging for you, then be ok with it. It is important that you navigate your partnership path and journey so that it aligns with your relationship values. Or else, you will always feel like a square trying to squeeze into a triangular whole. Good luck!

Chapter 2

Emotional associations that become lifelong patterns

What is an association? It is a mental connection between two events or feelings. For example, if talking to your father regularly results in you feeling hurt, then you might start making an association between your father (or a man) and expecting to feel hurt. An association can be caused by a single intense incident, or repeated stressors can reinforce it gradually.

A child's brain is programmed to make associations quickly. For example, the first time you put your hand on a hot stove, you get burned. You very quickly make an association and learn not to do that again. Your brain begins making associations at a very young age, well before you can walk and talk. These associations form your basic neural network or hard-wired patterns of thinking and behaviors that form your personality.

As important as associations are for your survival, they can also become destructive and detrimental to your health. That's because an association that is valid at one time (e.g., during abuse) is not necessarily helpful as an adult. A simplistic example would be an association of men with pain that might be helpful to a vulnerable five-year-old girl, but not so much to a lonely, single adult.

You make associations to avoid danger (as in the hot stove example) or to get your basic needs met. Think of a cat that is fed at a specific place and time of day—they will keep returning because they associate that person, place, and time with getting their needs met.

A child is seeking love and attention (a basic human need) and receives a beating instead, they may begin to develop an association between the need for love and the abuse they receive. They may also begin to associate bad behavior with getting attention. The child subconsciously adjusts their behavior to get more attention by misbehaving. Why? Because inappropriate behavior gets attention, attention gets punishment, and punishment is what they receive when they are seeking love. These concepts have become associated with the child's mind.

I am going to use my childhood as an example. When I needed love from my father, I experienced rejection and abandonment. I associated my need for love with abandonment. Whenever I needed love, I was rejected and abandoned. I attracted partners that would constantly reject me and abandon me when I sought love and acceptance. This pattern only came to a halt when I dealt with the underlying abuse issues. Now, when I want to be loved and accepted, that is exactly what I get.

Although these negative associations are well understood by therapists, the most common treatments are inappropriate. The biggest problem is that there are hundreds, perhaps thousands, of these associations made for each trauma. These are subconscious triggers relating to sights, smells, colors, etc. It is impossible to clear them all and for that reason it's appropriate to work with changing associations (or negative beliefs, which are associations expressed as words). The only safe and effective therapy is to clear the underlying trauma.

When you truly resolve the abuse trauma (truly resolve means you can no longer picture it in your mind and the charge has completely gone), the associations disappear. Yes, you can clear all negative associations or beliefs at once simply by resolving trauma. This is why I place such emphasis on resolving trauma in my workshops and guard people against working with symptoms alone, bypassing a trauma only causes it to resurface.

Environmental Triggers

Environmental triggers are a type of emotional association. In this case, the association is with something in your environment rather than another person. Everyday objects in your life can remind you of your abuse or negative experiences. This includes smells, sounds, or textures found in your living environment.

Phobias may stem from some level of abuse because the person may have made a negative association with the object that he or she has a fear of. I will give you some examples from clients.

Example One:

As a child, Anne was abused by her uncle. He would always hug and kiss her in an inappropriate way that would make her feel shameful and disgusted. As an adult, she experienced the same emotions of shame and disgust whenever her partner would hug and kiss her.

Example Two:

Betty was running home from school one day, laughing because her friend told her a joke. She was excited to share the joke with her father, who was mowing the lawn in front of the house. Betty ran into the yard and accidentally kicked a small pile of loose grass over the lawn that her father had just raked up. She started telling the joke to her dad with so much joy. Her father, however, was more frustrated about the mess that Betty made by kicking the pile of grass.

He yelled and smacked her. Betty started crying and felt very upset, invalidated, and traumatized by her father's unexpected reaction. Betty made a subconscious association with the smell of freshly cut grass and feeling insignificant. As an adult, every time she smells cut grass, her subconscious mind remembers the association she made. She felt upset, invalidated, and uncomfortable.

Sometimes the trigger can make you feel unsettled with no clear reason why especially if you cannot remember the association that you made.

Example 3:

John has a cat phobia. When John was a kindergartner, his teacher sexually abused him. There happened to be a cat in the room whilst he was being physically abused. His phobia of cats stemmed from this incident because of an environmental association between the cat and John's feelings of being scared, violated, and disrespected. On some level, it was easier to hold on to the negative feelings about cats than it was to remember the abuse. Every time John sees a cat in his environment, it triggers the feeling of being scared, violated and vulnerable. John had no conscious memory of the abuse until it came up in therapy.

Resolving the abuse trauma cleared the phobia and subsequent allergy.

I used to feel furious whenever I smelled alcohol, especially beer and brandy. I would feel angry, resentful, and stressed because of the associations that I made with these substances during my childhood. Alcohol was always present when I was abused by my grandparents and by my father. This created a very strong negative association.

When these types of associations are triggered, it can cause a great deal of anxiety. The anxiety results from not being able to identify why a person feels upset or bad when they smell/see/feel or hear something that may have subconsciously reminded them of a traumatic time in their life.

The only solution is to clear the underlying trauma. This raises the question "to what extent do you need to know about the abuse (especially suppressed or forgotten trauma) in order to clear it?" The answer is that it is possible to clear trauma without remembering it, provided the intention is to feel and process it. This important question is covered in more detail in our workshops and in my second book, Metaphysical Anatomy.

Chapter 3

Language for love

For human beings, one of the biggest blessings in life is love. Everyone agrees that one of the essential things in life is love, so happiness is closely related to receiving and giving love. "Love" is a wide range of powerful and pleasant emotional and mental experiences, including beautiful ideas, intense feelings of love for another person, and simple pleasures. No matter who we are, happiness can be found in love.

When love is so profound, why do we sometimes feel unhappy and disconnected in relationships that involve love? The answer to this question is straightforward. The reason why we feel disappointed and disconnected in our love relationships is not due to love itself. Instead, we become unhappy because we are unable to understand the love language of our partners.

We cannot match our love "vibes" with that of our partners. It is because we do not understand the way our partners love us. Not that our partners do not love us, but that sometimes our expectations of love are unrealistic or too high.

Let me explain. Have you ever thought your partner does not love you as much as you love them? I am sure the answer is yes. What if your relationship is doing relatively okay, but there is just that little something missing? You might feel that your partner does not love you anymore. Or maybe you think your partner does not show their love in a way that leaves you feeling fulfilled? Why? There is a simple answer to this.

People communicate and express their love for one another in different ways. In most cases, how someone speaks about love does not necessarily resonate with their partner. It is because they might have a different love language. One partner may say something, but the other hears something completely different, and they misinterpret their partner's actions.

As a fun example, we have antennas representing the brain. Each person's antenna has a radar, searching for a specific frequency of love. We then focus on our particular frequency, indicating what love should be and feel like. By becoming too tuned into our love frequency, we can overlook the love already present in our lives.

We cannot see, sense, or pick up the other love frequencies our partner might send us. Sometimes, we are not loved how we want to be loved. It can leave us feeling empty and unfulfilled. Yet we may have abundant love in our lives. We cannot see it because we are so focused on being loved in a specific way that we overlook and subconsciously ignore how much our partner loves us.

There are also situations where we enter relationships with too high or too many expectations. If our partner does not do certain things for us, we think our partner does not love us. However, in the meantime, our partner has a different language for love and communicates their love differently.

When we stop projecting what love should look like, we give our partners more emotional freedom to express themselves. As a result, we will be more receptive to their love language. Once an opportunity for emotional freedom, free of rigid love expression, beliefs, and values, has been created, there will be more room for growing together in spiritual, emotional, and mental ways instead of growing apart. Sometimes we become so comfortable and feel so safe with each other that we forget to go that extra mile to keep the flame burning.

Thinking that our partners do not love us because they do not do what our friend's partner does. People show love in ways that make them feel safe. We usually do not go outside our comfort zones when it comes to love. Why? Past traumas and disappointments often hold us back. Loving others means that we open ourselves to receive. For this reason, we might be a little reserved; unconsciously, we are trying to protect a fragile heart.

It is important to note that this does not apply to young couples only. I met people who have been married for 50 years. After all these years, they are still careful about how much they should allow themselves to love their spouse and how they show it. However, it does not necessarily mean that someone does not love us with all their heart.

Modern romantic movies have a lot to say. For the reader or viewer, romance novels and movies create unrealistic expectations about love. When we compare our love lives to films or books, we give our power away to these media publications. Most likely, our love life looks nothing like a recent movie we saw or a book we read. We eventually end up feeling empty, stuck, and unfulfilled. It is unfair for us to project such expectations onto our partners. If we do this, we set ourselves and our relationship up for failure. Instead, consider compromising with a partner; it is always a winner!

Another solution is to explain how we would feel if our partner could do something according to our preferences. Never telling your partner what they are doing is upsetting. Never blame your partner for not feeling loved enough.

Instead, look at the issue from a constructive angle and see where we can improve. Sometimes, we never know how valuable a diamond is until we lose it. Give your partner a chance to express themselves. It does not mean we have to change how we love someone. Adding a few extra chores or changing things that improve the relationship is always worthwhile, especially if we consider it a long-term relationship.

Ask your partner this simple question: "When do you love me the most?" If your partner's answer is within reason, do more of what your partner loves, and vice versa. Every relationship is a work in progress. Every day we can learn something new about a partner. How they feel and how they communicate their love. Be clear in your communications and what you want. Most importantly, ensure your antenna is in tune with picking up your partner's love signals.

Loving someone for all the wrong reasons

We have been blessed with one of the world's most beautiful emotions: the emotion of love. Love is significantly profound and unique.

It soothes and nourishes our souls and minds with positivity, comfort, and peace. It's challenging to live a happy life without it. Love has no boundaries, conditions, or impurities. If emotion is genuinely an emotion of love, it is always pure and unconditional if felt and projected with pure intentions.

However, sometimes people mistake their emotional, social, and physical needs for love. They think they love someone, but actually, they do not. They are only attached to someone because their needs are being fulfilled. Emotional or financial support is the most common example of such needs.

So, how can this conditional attachment for fulfilling needs be love? It is not love unless your definition of love is aligned with how your needs are met. So, it is always essential to understand whether an emotion is of love or something else.

We need to know how we misunderstand love with several other feelings. By understanding it, we will be able to figure out whether we love someone for all the right reasons or not.

We never start a relationship to break it. We set out with the best intentions. We try to overcome any initial disagreements or problems. However, when time passes and the relationship does not improve, we may stay stuck out of fear of failure. How can we determine if we are staying with our partner for the wrong reasons?

Love is a complex topic because we all have different values and beliefs. What we think is true love is something completely different from other people. Sometimes, we might "love" someone out of fear. It is true if we had a partner who was raised in stressful circumstances during their childhood. I knew I "loved" my father out of fear as a child. My dad only noticed me when I did something wrong. Even though he gave me negative attention, my need to be acknowledged by him was at least met. My need for love was met by adverse and even abusive reactions.

It is like being programmed with incorrect reference points due to trauma. Compare this situation to linking wires in a machine but with faulty wiring connections—the device will not explode, yet it will not work very well either. For me, attention and love from my dad were equivalent to abuse, anger, and aggression. This was my definition of love throughout my relationships.

If such a pattern of punishment in response to the need for love persists, a child will start associating lousy behavior with attention. Sadly, this child is not experiencing a positive reaction from one or both parents and others. The child usually accepts this type of reaction from the parent. This destructive association tends to play out later in adulthood, causing relationship conflicts. This negative association also affects their ability to love others for all the right reasons and not out of fear of punishment, loneliness, or rejection.

A child instinctively relies on their parents for shelter, food, and safety. During the child's formative years, they "love" the parents because their basic survival needs are met by them. Loving someone sounds better in our conscious mind than acknowledging the reality of a deteriorating relationship or facing our worst fears, like loneliness, abandonment, or rejection.

The emotional reward of plainly being with someone instead of being alone can sometimes outweigh all common logic, especially if we are in an unhealthy relationship. We know we might be in an unhealthy relationship but are too scared to do something about it.

It feels safer being with someone rather than being alone. It is not love. It is a fear of abandonment and loneliness disguised as love. If we are affected by this situation, we tend to misinterpret our circumstances.

The comfort, emotional reward, and safety received from being with someone fulfil a basic need—the need to be part of something, whether it is a relationship, community, or family.

We have the instinct to feel safe and find safety in numbers or complete isolation. Here we are looking for comfort in others, such as a partner. When someone fulfils our need for safety and basic needs (such as a lovely house, food, money, and clothing), we tend to react to this partner from a deep instinctual level.

One partner covers the other's needs. However, it is here that we confuse feeling safe and cared for with the feeling of being loved. Yes, we may give and do things for others because we love them, but we also fulfil an instinctual need to provide. Looking for and receiving items is deeply programmed into our biology, ensuring biological and emotional survival.

Sometimes we confuse the fulfilment of these instinctual needs with being loved. We realize this situation where our partner is physically or emotionally abusive.

Although this is not the case for everyone, it is the case for most people in unhappy relationships. Now the big question is, what is love?

What is it supposed to feel like? How do we know that we love someone for all the right reasons? The answer?

Imagine taking away your fear of loneliness and resolving your abandonment trauma. Now add a house, enough food, enough money, and feelings of safety and security in your environment.

Imagine these can never be taken away from you. Would you still want to be with your partner if you had all this?

Chapter 4

Anger versus boundaries

Getting angry is a natural, instinctual reaction to danger. We need some amount of anger in order to survive. Anger may be a powerful motivator for bringing about positive change. However, letting it take control of us can result in harmful, destructive behaviors like emotional, verbal, or even physical violence and abuse in relationships. Moreover, the most important thing to consider here is why sometimes anger is necessary. What role does anger play in our lives? How can anger be useful? There can be different aspects where anger is necessary, but what I love the most is that it helps us develop our emotional, psychological, and physical boundaries. These boundaries act like guardians to ensure our emotional, physical, and psychological safety. In this way, you can see that some amount of anger is necessary for survival. Let's see in detail how anger helps us to establish our boundaries.

If you do not have healthy boundaries or you do not know what your boundaries are, then how will you recognize them? How are other people even going to recognize your boundaries? So how other people respect you reflects how well you can establish your boundaries. In such cases, when you are not clear, there are no clear conscious and subconscious projections or guidelines regarding what you will tolerate and not tolerate. People can take advantage of you in such scenarios.

At this moment, boundaries are shown through body language and verbal communication. For example, if you have trouble communicating, you will have poor boundaries. You will even have poor personal boundaries because it has a big ripple effect and often does not have a good ending. If there is no clear line of where and how far something or someone can push you, then the chances of people disrespecting you are much higher. So, the most challenging aspect is not even knowing where your boundaries are.

Now that begs the question, "why would you use anger to establish an emotional or physical boundary?" The reason is that you may have experienced emotional or physical abuse. So, the wounded, suppressed, or traumatized part of you is so saturated with feeling powerless, vulnerable, and unsafe that anger has now become your boundary. It has become the tool you use to access this emotional state that makes you feel confident and strong. Thus, you use anger to express an opinion, a threshold, or an emotion you normally would not have been able to express.

Anger also serves to show you that a boundary has been crossed. When your boundary is overstepped, you normally get angry and feel resentful. However, the anger and resentment were delayed responses, showing that your boundaries were crossed long ago. It means that you missed that trigger point that was crossed by someone too late. You did not act quickly enough to stop the boundary failure because you didn't recognize it.

Why did you fail to recognize it? It could be that you were not allowed to have these physical, and emotional boundaries and the space you needed as a child to practice your boundaries in a safe way. You could not speak your truth and express your voice or your opinion. Perhaps you could not express how uncomfortable or disrespected you felt in the past. So, all these factors could be unresolved wounds from your past that cause a certain level of numbness resulting in you perhaps failing to recognize when boundaries were being crossed.

Let's also look at when anger and aggression become false confidence. In this case, aggression is an accumulation of many boundaries overstepped in the past, and you have now reached your limit. Usually, in most cases, it is subconscious because you are so used to automatically suppressing how you feel that you do not consciously realize how you are layering up these suppressed emotions. So, you reach your limit regarding what you will tolerate and what you will not. The end results? You might be sensitive to your boundaries being overstepped, causing knee-jerk reactions with messy endings.

You will notice that it is much easier to say no when you are really upset, rather than when you are in a good and happy state. So, aggression is not confidence; it is an overcorrection of overstepped boundaries. Sometimes we completely surrender and do not even try to establish a boundary. The will to establish boundaries may have been completely wiped out; that is where the danger lies. It is because someone who is exhausted and drained from absorbing abuse, wrath, or intimidation also has limitations. It typically can happen when the victim becomes the abuser because they observe the aggressor and their behavior and see the unhealthy benefit of being angry.

When this person was angry, you probably noticed they were listened to and respected, but they were respected out of fear and not because they were appreciated. You might also have noticed that they did things they normally would not have done if they were not so angry or aggressive. Now this pattern will only set you up for a very lonely life and potentially just people who love you out of fear and not for the sake of love itself.

It was the same pattern for me as well. I noticed this pattern in my relationship, especially in my friendship dynamics. So, you will never find the happiness and peace you are most likely searching for because anger is the opposite vibration of happiness. Anger traps you in a state of mind that only holds grudges and resentment. It will ultimately disconnect you from your true, authentic self, meant to be peaceful and in sync with your present life, future, friends, love, family, and higher purpose.

It is also important to explore your associations while setting boundaries. Do you use anger to express boundaries? Do you use aggression? Do you use resentment, rigidity, resistance, or stubbornness to set boundaries? These tactics are only causing more problems. Why? They are robbing you of your joy and a positive quality of life. It's hard to be happy when you are upset all the time.

Now, what would be a great exercise for you is to look at what you feel when you express a boundary. Look at the emotions that you feel. Look at potential root causes as to why you would feel these emotions. Do the emotions you are feeling correlate with the situation you are dealing with? Or is the situation being misunderstood due to old traumas resurfacing and triggering new feelings in you, making you feel this way and causing you to relapse into an angry state? So, it would be a good point for you to look at.

Now I will give you a completely different perspective in terms of conscious awareness of anger when you actually need to express a boundary. So, when you feel that rage coming up, explore it because it is there to tell you that an old wound is now being poked at. Sometimes it can be an innocent person accidentally doing or saying something that hurt you. However, the intention is not to hurt you. So, in that case, please take a deep breath, feel the rage, and be aware of it.

Most importantly, be okay with the fact that it is there because the worst thing you can do is try to fight and resist feeling it. When you resist feeling it, you will feel even angrier because you are making yourself wrong for feeling a valid and real feeling. The reaction is there; however, you try to convince yourself that it is not there when you know it is. You are just trying to fool yourself, which is making you angry.

Be okay with the anger being there. Firstly, if you are in doubt about what is going on, are you now being taken advantage of? Is there something within you being triggered? Take a deep breath and feel the rage. It is like you give the rage a voice at that moment. Rage will give you a message that you will emotionally feel. Listen to that message. Whatever that message tells you, it will bring you one step closer to whether how you feel is out of context or is a recognition of an overstepped boundary between you and someone else.

Boundaries are still significant in terms of how your boundaries are crossed and how you will respond subsequently. It is because you will establish a boundary at such a moment.

Get clarity on why you feel the way you do so that your reaction and response can be balanced within the context of the overstepped boundary.

Boundaries, dating, and relationships

Boundaries are crucial to leading a healthy and happy life, particularly when it comes to dating and love relationships. Clear, healthy boundaries can prevent a relationship from ending, ultimately, or deteriorating into something harmful and toxic. Although relationships can be fascinating, we must understand what boundaries are and why they are essential. Boundaries are restrictions we place on how other people can distract us or interact with us.

We are more likely to feel heard, acknowledged, and loved when our partners respect our boundaries. So, they will never take us for granted. Moreover, boundaries reveal our identity in relationships for what we are. Having healthy boundaries in relationships that involve love includes taking responsibility for our feelings. It also promotes mutual relevance, respect, and care in a dating relationship.

Healthy boundaries encourage our partners and us to consider each other's feelings, get one other's consent, and express gratitude. If we do not set clear and healthy boundaries in our relationships, we cannot respect our partner's activities and their ideas and viewpoints. Unfortunately, we sometimes do not realize the importance of having boundaries in relationships. We might blindly keep investing our valuable time and energy in a toxic relationship and end up severely emotionally and psychologically distressed. Therefore, we must see the importance of setting clear boundaries in our love relationships. These boundaries will help us realize whether we are dating for all the right reasons or all the wrong ones.

Dating for all the right reasons versus dating for all the wrong reasons

We think we love someone, but subconsciously, we are afraid of being alone. In our conscious mind, falling in love with someone sounds better than admitting that our relationship is getting worse or facing our worst fears, like being alone, abandoned, or rejected.

Sometimes, especially in a toxic relationship, the emotional benefits of being with someone rather than alone overshadow all logical considerations. We know that our relationship is unhealthy, but we fear taking action. We feel safer when we are with someone, compared to when we are alone. It is not love at all. It is just our fear of being alone and abandoned that misconstrues it as love. We might think we love someone but are still with them because we do not want to be alone. It is because being with someone comforts us, and gives us emotional rewards and a sense of safety. It fulfills our basic need: the need to be a part of something, whether it is a family, a relationship, or a group.

We all have a natural need to feel safe. We feel secure in groups or when we are entirely alone. This discussion focuses on finding comfort and peace in others, such as a partner. When our safety and basic needs (such as food, a pleasant home, and clothing) are met by our partners, we respond to them on a primal level.

One partner fulfills the needs of the other. Here, however, we misinterpret feelings of safety and care with feelings of love. The motivation behind helping others may be love, but it also satisfies a natural desire. We are biologically wired to seek out and get things. It is necessary for both our emotional and physical survival. We frequently confuse the fulfillment of these innate desires with being loved.

However, we realize this when our partners emotionally, mentally, or physically hurt us. It is not true for everyone, but it is unquestionably true for most people in unpleasant relationships. Now we must answer the critical question: "What is love? How is it supposed to make us feel? How can we be sure that we are in love with someone for the right reasons? What is the answer to this crucial question?

Even I need to think about this. However, there are a few questions we can ask ourselves to help us answer it:

- Imagine being free from the fear of being alone.
- You overcome the trauma of being abandoned.
- Add enough money, enough food, a home, and a sense of security in your surroundings now.
- Imagine that you can never lose these.

Would you still want to remain with your partner if you had everything on the list, as mentioned above? We frequently fall in love with the notion that someone can satisfy our needs, which can lead to an attraction motivated by need rather than love. We think our partners can give us everything we lack in life. True deep love rarely results from this kind of attraction; instead, it frequently develops into a co-dependent relationship.

There might be a part of us that can identify with this. We might be the one who needs to be rescued deep down. Or, maybe we are the one who needs saving and views a relationship as a haven that may help us escape difficult circumstances and experiences. We frequently glamorize a relationship and believe that our love may rescue and restore a man or woman who is having trouble with their personal or professional life or finances.

We may want to be with someone because we do not want to confront the emotional demons that emerge when we are alone. Ultimately, it is not about disliking ourselves, but about how loneliness makes us feel. Since such emotions may be so powerful when there is no diversion from them, we link them with ourselves and our identities.

We may believe that we can assist our partners in getting back on their feet, but if we have weak boundaries in our relationships, things can go catastrophically wrong. We engage in relationships because we do not want to tackle our fears alone and because we can draw others into our troubles and difficulties. If we do not correctly communicate our boundaries in these situations, we can find ourselves dealing with an issue that is more serious than the one we had before we started dating.

We must understand that boundaries are significant, especially when figuring out what we want in our relationships. For example, we may wish to engage in a relationship hoping that it will help us heal. However, the relationship is likely to fail in circumstances without clear and healthy boundaries. The relationship will just soothe us and cover the intense suffering we have not dealt with.

Sometimes, weak boundaries and a fear of loneliness can lead to a relationship dynamic that leaves us feeling:

- That we will tolerate disrespectful behavior from others.
- We are changing our personality and values to improve our relationship with the other person.
- We are settling for considerably less than we deserve in the relationship because we are not monitoring what we deserve.
- We stick to a relationship despite knowing it will fail, expecting it will succeed if we invest more effort and time.
- We are excessively controlling the other person since we do not want to lose them.

It is normal to gravitate into toxic relationships, especially if we have a history of doing so or have seen our parents engaging in such behavior. Instead of stepping into the unknown and not knowing what to expect, we tend to stick with what we are familiar with. Our subconscious mind wants to feel more at ease with abusive dynamics if we are used to being mistreated, insulted, and having our boundaries crossed. No matter how unhealthy or toxic the relationship is, we already have ingrained survival strategies that enable us to deal with the stress, pressure, control, intimidation, and routine testing of our boundaries.

Even if we attract a healthy relationship, we can still struggle with trust because we might think that the other person is hiding an aggressor behind their "apparent face" and that this is too good to be true. Even so, not everyone intends to step over our limits and take advantage of us; there are also some remarkable individuals in the world.

"Take someone who doesn't keep score, who's not looking to be richer, or afraid of losing, who has not the slightest interest even in his own personality: he's free." — *Jalaluddin Rumi*

True love versus friendship

Indeed, I have also experienced this. In my case, I realized that I had a crush on someone. We were not close friends, though. When we first started dating, there was no genuine friendship. At the start of the relationship, I was confident that I liked him because he was the ideal partner for me—almost like what we would see in a movie. I was not aware at the time that I was captivated by him because of who I believed he was and what I thought he could become.

I understood that I had imagined him based on what I had seen on television and what I had read in romance books. He appeared to have treated me in the same way. This idealization is significantly more prevalent than you would imagine! It is frequently harmful, although it can also be good at times. When you meet someone new, especially for the first time, like on a blind date, you may idealize them. It is because idealization fills in those parts of the person you are still trying to learn and understand and eliminates any imperfections in them. Especially in the initial stages of a new relationship, admiration may knock down our common sense. It is precisely what happened in my case.

We both ended up putting unreasonable expectations on one other, making the relationship highly frustrating as we tried to make it work. However, because I did not want to transform into what he desired me to become, and he did not wish to transform into the person I was expecting him to become, we ended up despising one another. Also, the friendship part was missing and not thriving. His ego prevented him from talking to me more about what friends would say or do.

I never saw a side of him that would have made me consider him a friend in addition to a lover. I soon became aware of how lonely I was. We were not growing together, and the friendship was gone. Although both of us feared being alone, we lost contact. After five years of dating, he asked me to marry him. I replied, "Yes" before realizing what I had said. After three months of being engaged, I finally understood that I was not respecting my beliefs and boundaries regarding what I wanted in a relationship or marriage. We both felt relieved when I called off the engagement because we knew it was the best move for our futures.

For me, this relationship was quite significant. It taught me what I did not want in a relationship. The difficulties and challenging times overshadowed the relationship's good points. That was a strong indication that it was moving in the wrong direction. I understood that boundaries, realistic expectations, and restrictions are also necessary for a relationship, and I realized that I had disregarded each of them.

After my breakup, I had to reconsider my limits, expectations, and boundaries. I also recognized why I was attracted to that person. He was a pure reflection of my father, a brash, unreliable, dishonest alcoholic who laid the blame for his issues on everyone.

I had things to check. I started by examining the associations that a relationship had brought with it. In my case, I realized that a relationship with a man implies mistreatment, being deceived, a lack of communication, being treated more like a servant than a partner, putting the partner's needs ahead of mine, and sacrificing my objectives and needs to meet his.

I do not blame that person. He was undoubtedly attracted to me. I was captivated by him because he reflected the dynamics with my father. It almost felt like a match made in hell! I took complete responsibility for my role in this. I continued to encourage him and his dominating, demanding behavior. I was too young to understand that I deserved a better relationship.

"Be grateful for whoever comes, because each has been sent as a guide from beyond." — Jalaluddin Rumi

My journey toward healing primarily began here. I understood that I needed to change these patterns, improve my self-esteem, and reevaluate my beliefs and boundaries. I had unconsciously adopted my mother's values (in terms of what a wife should be— and I have to give it to my mother that she gave the marriage her best!). Moreover, most partners in several parts of the world struggle with poor self-esteem because there is a strong belief that the other partner are the leaders, and the rest of the family members are just followers. Anyone who crosses this line of belief will suffer consequences. It was back then, in the 1980s and 1990s. Finally, things were improving. I overcame my problems with relationships. I also reassessed my thresholds, expectations, and relationship boundaries.

How can we determine if someone in a relationship is crossing our boundaries? I established the threshold level:

- When someone yells at us.
- When we are given instructions without consideration for our needs or well-being by the person giving the instructions.
- When we have to stop what we are doing to help someone reach their goals while we are working on ours.
- When we cannot wear the clothes, we want to wear, etc.

Now, I would like you to make your list.

How do you determine if you are not being acknowledged and valued in your relationship? Make your list; set your threshold limit.

The table below is just a draft sample to get you started.

Rough Draft	Most important to least
	1
	2

Note the boundary or threshold that is clear as you look at the second column of this list. What emotions does that limit evoke in you? If it is accompanied by trauma and stress, I strongly advise you to relieve the stress behind this border because it is powerful enough to be at the top of your list. This boundary, particularly the fundamental stress connected to it, is frequently a subconscious motivator that can either be beneficial or even lead to self-sabotage.

"Be melting snow. Wash yourself of yourself." — Jalaluddin Rumi, the Essential Rumi

Furthermore, it is critical to consider your feelings and explaining your boundaries to your partner. When you expressed your boundaries, how were you treated? I will give another example from my life. In the past, I associated setting boundaries with fear of conflict, rejection, being threatened with abandonment, attachment, abuse, etc.

Make a list since it will help you better understand which fears prevent you from setting boundaries:

Communicating my boundaries to my partner =

_____

You might be feeling much better now that the exercise is over. Your self-confidence, respect, and faith in yourself will grow as you become more transparent and aware of what inspires you and the obstacles that lie behind the conflicts within your boundaries.

What you expect from a relationship can also be a part of boundaries. In other words, it is a deal breaker if they lack certain traits. It is crucial to list the behaviors or characteristics you can accept within a partner.

Let's begin with deal-breakers. Here are a few instances:

- Whether they have a drug problem.
- Aggression issues
- Warning signals of future violence.
- Lies and deception
- Lack of consistency in their beliefs and belief system.
- Mood swings that are attributed to us and make us feel guilty.
- Feeling obligated to ensure this person's fulfilment.
- Feeling to abandon your principles and values to conform to this individual's beliefs and values.
- Being asked to stop spending time with my friends.

Now make your list.

What are deal breakers in a relationship?

The table below is just a draft sample to get you started.

Rough Draft	Most important to least
	1
	2

Make a list of the compromises you can make. Here are a few instances:

- They might be disorganized.
- They sometimes forget important dates, like your birthday (this has happened to almost everyone).
- They are attempting to appear more powerful than they are to impress you.
- Avoiding closeness; when they get to know you better, this inclination frequently disappears.
- Being too organized and wanting to do everything correctly.

Start making your list now. There is no need to rank the above compromises from most important to least important in this activity.

Moreover, making a list of characteristics you would like your partner to have is the last activity. Be reasonable in your expectations. Keep in mind that everyone has flaws and personality quirks, including you. That is why you made a list of what you can accept.

Here are a few instances:

- Being humorous
- Able to maintain communication even during challenging moments.
- They are capable of supporting you just as much as you support them.
- Being truthful
- Respect the values of loyalty.

- Cooperation, etc.

Qualities you would like your partner to have. However, from a different perspective, this is still a part of your boundaries:

Rough Draft   **Most important to least**

The table below is just a draft sample to get you started.

	1
	2

Important things to keep in mind: Be a partner, not a parent! When you consider dating in its larger context, you realize that it ultimately comes down to satiating your need for friendship, love, and acceptance. However, the emotional factors underlying this need and desire can make it healthy or unhealthy. Understanding the prior exercises will help you better understand why you are looking for that particular person.

You have a greater chance of finding the right partner after these obstacles are removed. You give too much of yourself in a relationship that quickly drains you when there is an unclear line between your boundaries and how you communicate them. You realize that you have remained optimistic only to learn that the other person has abusing your kindness.

Your love and capacity to love are intrinsic to who you are. You want to share this side of yourself with someone who will accept it and return the energy to you in their unique way. The energy in a relationship always flows when there is an equal amount of give and take. It establishes a secure space where two people may connect, cooperate, and work independently while maintaining their uniqueness and freedom.

You have no obligation or duty to guide or heal another person. Each person manages their healing process and has the option to change or not. Nobody will purposefully search for someone to challenge them and make them unhappy. Nobody truly goes out looking for someone to break their boundaries. Although when we first meet someone, love can impair our judgement.

If you go into a relationship with the idea that you can help or save the other person, think again. You do not just enter a relationship; you enter a project construction site. Making the other person feel that there is always something wrong with them and that they are not good enough can only result in resentment, anger, and emotional distress, which can then progress to abusive words and even actions. This type of relationship dynamic will fail 100% of the time. This individual can even become so reliant on you that you eventually end up with a partner who is inferior to you rather than one who is equal to you.

"Yesterday I was clever, so I wanted to change the world. Today I am wise, so I am changing myself." — Jalaluddin Rumi

Be Honest

Share your expectations for a relationship with your partner openly and sincerely. If you can get your partner to create a list similar to yours, you can exchange them and discuss any significant differences. The golden rule is always to be truthful.

Do not compromise your principles or boundaries because they could contradict your partner's. That is why you initially conducted this exercise with them, to resolve disagreements before they become an issue. Usually, we can resolve these disagreements respectfully and without arguing.

"Raise your words, not voice. It is rain that grows flowers, not thunder."— Jalaluddin Rumi

If, however, a boundary value at the bottom of the list becomes a deal breaker for you (for instance, if you value faithfulness above all else and your partner is open to casual relationships), then your relationship is not right for you. You will eventually hate your partner because you are now sacrificing a significant part of yourself and your values. You will pay for your sacrifice in the end. Your identity and self-esteem will suffer significantly as a result, and you might find yourself starting over. Therefore, I cannot stress this enough: maintain your boundaries and be faithful to your partners! They are there to assist you in determining the right relationship that will benefit your present and future.

Always be up forward and honest about your intentions for the relationship. Are you seeking a long-term relationship or do you merely want to stay in the dating stage? To avoid hurting yourself or others, be honest with your limits and communication. Additionally, especially in a new relationship, be honest about intimacy. People are frequently intimate on the first date in today's modern society, but this is not always the case. You do not have to follow the majority; respect yourself and your body if you want to set an intimacy limit; you have every right to do so.

When opposites attract

It occurs when we meet someone with a quality, we lack so strongly that we immediately fall in love with them, forgetting possibly the other 95% of our incompatibilities.

Here are a few instances:

- We are fragile. Our partner is strong.
- Our partner is wealthy. We enjoy overspending.
- Our partner is an excellent provider. We hardly manage to pay our bills.
- Our partner is such a fantastic communicator. We are unable to speak clearly.
- Our partner makes us complete.

We face a very high risk of getting dependent on the other person when we enter a relationship of this kind. They will emphasize our inadequacies and make us feel like we cannot survive without them. However, we can find ourselves in a loveless position when things become rough, and we finally recognize that this relationship is founded on our unsatisfied desires. Never ignore these warning signs because doing so could lead to a very short fairy tale with a possibly unpleasant ending.

Boundaries are fundamental in relationships; the only way you can establish them is by getting to know yourself first.

Chapter 5

Fighting and arguing- finding common

Conflicts can happen when people have different ideas or beliefs that contradict each other. Sometimes people misunderstand one another and jump to incorrect assumptions, which can lead to conflict. If disagreements are not addressed peacefully, they may lead to arguments and hatred.

It is common to disagree with others sometimes. Even occasional arguments are a normal part of family life. We do not always agree with everything when speaking with our parents or friends. We are all naturally different, so we see and believe things differently. It does not imply that agreeing or treating others respectfully is impossible. However, a persistent argument may be unpleasant and harmful to relationships.

We can share the same viewpoint with another person if we identify some common ground. Then, it becomes easier to find common ground on other things we previously had no agreement on. It does not mean that we will disregard our viewpoint, or the other person will. Communicating positively can help avoid conflict so people can find a peaceful resolution. Finding common ground is sometimes the only way to deal with challenging conversations.

One of several reasons people fight and argue is the lack of common ground and a difference in opinion. The common ground is where we meet other people halfway. People fight because they want to be heard. There is a need within us to have our opinions acknowledged, respected, and understood. When our values and truth are not heard satisfactorily, we become defensive and angry. Our self-worth and values feel invalidated.

Conversations can then escalate to an argument as we fight for our values and truth to be respected. Although some people may suffice with having their values and truth respected, others may feel more validated and important when they fight and argue.

Healthy debates are acceptable. However, we look at deeper unresolved issues when things get out of hand.

When someone becomes too rigid, aggressive, and abusive, they display overcompensation for lack of acknowledgment. This lack of acknowledgment often goes back to their childhood when their truth and opinions may have been squashed and ignored. As children, their values and ideas may even have been punished. The unconscious mind remembers what happened in the past.

Are these children who have now become adults who are overly aggressive people gearing themselves up to defend their truth the same way they had to defend it during childhood? Sometimes, these individuals can become abusive in their attempt to deflect and throw you off-topic. At this point, you are getting too close to something they are protecting.

The fear of not being heard and understood is another explanation for aggressive behavior. When the truth is not acknowledged, feelings of rejection appear. In most cases, when someone feels this way, they become aggressive to protect their vulnerable heart and emotional state. Anger is now used as a source of power.

In a state of anger, it is easier for them to say what they have been suppressing. You know how easy it is to say how you feel when you are upset, right? I acknowledge, though, that someone's childhood trauma should never be an excuse for becoming aggressive. People who argue based on childhood trauma are stuck in a time-lapse. They have not learned how to let go, move forward, and treat every situation as a new and clean slate.

People who argue uncontrollably may have seen a parent behave this way. Consequently, this seemed to be a "good" way to force your values and opinions onto others. People stuck in this behavior pattern will continue playing out this pattern, even when they realize it is causing more distress and tension for both parties. Often, we must make a conscious choice to change this type of behavior. In a state of anger, we rarely care about the consequences of our words and actions until later when the consequences stare us in the face. Some people learn that through stubbornness and anger, things that need to be said can be said. They also learn that calmness and politeness do not get them anywhere. Their anger serves and helps them; they hold on to their anger. Anger stimulates them to take certain types of actions in which they otherwise do not have confidence.

People who rely on angry behavior feel safe with what they know and how they communicate it. The more others challenge how this person communicates, the more the person relying on anger will dig their heels in. For anger-driven people, the way they communicate has served them positively in the past; they will therefore hold on to these communication patterns and rigid values.

When someone's opinion is not respected according to their need for it to be respected, they feel exposed and humiliated and become defensive. So, another argument starts. This cycle stops when the aggressive opponent desires to change their ways.

The aggressive opponent must look deeper to understand why they behave in specific ways. What are the reasons for their fierce value and truth defenses? Has something happened to them in the past? How did influential people (such as parents, friends, and family) react in response to them raising their opinions and truths? Did they come from a background where children should be seen and not heard? The aggressive opponent must face the question: when will they let go of their unjust childhood treatment and move on? In answering these questions, you will understand why a partner, friend, or family member responds to differences in opinion in specific ways.

Let's explore how you can seek understanding and resolve these challenges. The best approach is to place yourself in the aggressive opponent's shoes. What are they feeling? Can you understand how they feel? Let's forget for a second what has been said in the argument. Ask yourself, how does this person feel? Now, rewind and focus on what has been said in the argument. Can you match their words with their feelings? Usually, you cannot match feelings with words. The aggressive opponent wants to say something else but does not know how.

This is merely to give you a glimpse of what could potentially take place in their mind at the time of conflict.

Understanding this first step resolves confusion, anger, and feelings of attack. This person feels challenged by what they need to say. For example, anger outbursts show the person's fears of losing control of a situation or person. Because of their disempowered feelings, they access their anger to give them the confidence to say what needs to be said. Anger can be a sign of frustration or boundary failure. Usually, aggressive opponents are angrier with themselves than anyone else; unfortunately, this anger is projected onto you or others.

The second step in resolving arguments is to find common ground. Common ground is the mid-point in opinion differences—where you and your partner can meet halfway. You must find a part of your truth or opinion that the other person understands, no matter how small. Likewise, your partner should find a part of their truth or opinion that you know and agree with. The argument is resolved by reaching this common ground point; the rest is irrelevant.

It is not possible to always agree with everyone on everything; know that this is reasonable. Just because there is a disagreement between you and another party does not mean the conflict should escalate into an argument. When the debate escalates into an argument, you are fighting about more than just a misunderstood opinion. You are fighting for your emotional needs that were not met during childhood by your guardian. You are fighting to be heard, understood, and validated. If your disagreement escalates into an argument, know that unexpressed frustrations are surfacing.

When you feel at ease with your beliefs, difference in opinion should not affect you. After all, you know who you are and what you stand for. Why do you need the approval of others? Answering this question reveals a lot about why you or someone else feels so upset when there is a difference in opinion. Treading too close to something the aggressive opponent does not want to reveal to you can trigger aggressive behavior. The aggressive opponent deflects by becoming abusive, distracting you from the vulnerability that they are feeling. They might fear being exposed, vulnerable, controlled, and humiliated.

It is acceptable to disagree!

There are many reasons we argue. It is acceptable to disagree. What is important here is that you find common ground where you can meet each other halfway, leaving you and your partner, friend, or family member feeling understood, heard, and acknowledged. After all, feeling accepted already takes away a great deal of anger, frustration, and rejection feelings. In an argument, saying, "I acknowledge how you feel and what you just said," will already release 70% of the tension!

There are also times when disagreements become too intensive and too regular. Due to these injustices and unresolved issues, people may go their separate ways, which can be acceptable. However, only move away from this person or situation for the right reasons and nothing else. Never walk away from a person or situation because you are running from something you do not want to deal with. Whatever you are running away from will only manifest in a new relationship, friendship, or family member.

Never start the blame game.

People must never blame one another; blaming is not acceptable. Blaming causes more trouble and confrontation. By blaming, you are giving the other person a reason to become defensive. In their minds, you are giving them a valid reason to attack and blame you for specific issues verbally.

The best way to express this is by starting the sentence with, "I feel…. when you do [this]." By starting your sentence with "I feel," you are not attacking someone's actions. Thus, the person cannot deny feelings even if they deny their actions. Always say how the person's actions affected you. Never blame them. The moment you blame them, they shut down, and arguments start. The selective hearing kicks in, and they hear what they want to hear—i.e., they only hear and experience you attacking them. They will not hear the real reason for the discussion.

What did you say?

I have learned that 80% of my disagreements are resolved when I ask the other person to repeat what they think I said. Repeating what you think someone said can already resolve many issues and miscommunications. We sometimes have selective hearing when we feel threatened, verbally attacked, or blamed. Your focus is so attuned to specific keywords that when you hear those keywords, everything else that is being said becomes redundant. Your brain filters out essential information because you are focusing on keywords, keywords that make you experience an attack. There may be keywords that unconsciously give you a reason to become defensive.

So, next time you are arguing, try to understand why the person said what they said. Did they use the sledgehammer effect, saying harsh things to hurt and distract you from coming too close to their vulnerabilities? Or are they trying to say something else? Do some introspection as well. Do you understand what you are trying to say? What kind of outcome do you want from a disagreement? When you have these answers, work towards achieving this in your disagreement discussion. Set yourself an intention, have a goal with the debate, and work towards it.

Never project.

Never allow others to project their beliefs onto you, intending to sway you away from what you believe in. People can share their opinions, and so can you. There is a difference between sharing and projecting. We should never demean others for believing in something that we might not understand, appreciate, or value the same way they do. The other person's beliefs and values serve them in one way or another.

Using a personal example of disagreements. I am very time orientated. Due to my busy schedule, I have learned to pick my disagreements. I value my time, and there are times when a disagreement (this is the actual disagreement, not the person with whom I disagree) is not worthy of my time. Instead, I acknowledge what the person said and respond, "You have every right to believe that because it is your truth, and I respect it." Such a response validates what the other person said, preventing feelings of rejection.

People with a tendency to argue are very rigid about their values and beliefs; compromising is challenging for them and often because of bad associations with compromising. Having too much time can also lead to more arguments! I have told a few people who like to argue, "Why don't you just get an extra job to keep yourself busy? You seem to have too much free time on your hands." Their reactions were always very entertaining, but they could lead to another argument, which you are trying to avoid.

The price you pay for being the peacekeeper

We experience a great deal of challenges in life. We go through various social, emotional, mental, and physical stages in life. We are all aware that every part of life has a negative side. We put a lot of effort into reaching certain milestones during our lives.

Love, preserving relationships, and simply surviving are milestones for different people. For others, it's money. However, some people put a lot of effort into achieving something valuable and universal to all these milestones. It is a peaceful mind and a peacekeeping nature.

Peace has always been important. We are willing to do anything for peace. Due to our peacekeeping nature, we escape insanity to have a peaceful mind, whether by going on vacation or moving away from a toxic environment.

We try our best to maintain peace in every situation. We always avoid any conflicting problems. We sometimes want peace so badly that we even ignore unjustified criticism, bullying, and aggression from abusers.

We do not speak up for our rights and avoid bullies because we want to avoid drama or frustrating scenarios. It all starts with many emotional, mental, and social reasons that upset us, and we all feel the need to escape for our own and others' peace.

Peacekeeping is an excellent quality to have. But sometimes, we have to pay a high price for it because we enable the abusers to bully us. Peacekeeping habits can make us victims of manipulation and aggression.

Are you a peacekeeper? Do you know someone who feels it is their role to be the peacekeeper in the family? We all love peace and quietness, but sometimes people sacrifice their truth and right to be respected for peace in their life and environment.

Often, there are two possible peacemaker roles, and this is when a peacekeeper can balance a confronting situation and help everyone involved to see things clearly, rather than reacting from a place of anger.

This peacemaking approach is healthy. The second peacemaker role is noted when we always try to keep the peace when an abuser becomes angry and verbally abusive. In this case, the peacekeeper's mediating role becomes redundant. The peacemaker's role becomes an enabling one. Let me explain this point.

Let's say you had a partner who would become strict if they did not get what they wanted. Nobody ever stood up to them. The partner would create drama, and everyone would drop everything and respond to their needs. If someone dares to challenge them, they will receive verbal punishment and rejection. The familiar shame and guilt trip is the result of challenging this partner.

If you point out how inappropriate their behavior is, it is denied. The outcome is that you are given the cold shoulder. At this point, she manipulates others into believing she is the victim. However, since you adopted the peacemaker role, you do not say anything and forgive her behavior. You may excuse her behavior, saying she may have had a challenging past. She is in pain and has a reason for being manipulative, mean, and a bully.

Looking at this example, let's explore how the peacekeeper can become the enabler. Firstly, the partner is getting a huge benefit or secondary gain from their behavior. No one challenges them when they become abusive or express unnecessarily harsh words. Secondly, they have no reason to take responsibility for their behavior and situation. There is no encouragement for them to deal with unresolved issues, contributing to their anger and frustration. It is easier to release anger onto an innocent person than to go down memory lane to resolve old patterns and emotional blocks.

Most importantly, the partner cannot admit their problem. As long as they are being enabled or validated to abuse or argue, it is evident that the one complaining is the one with the problem. In this case, you are the peacemaker. Suddenly, you are the one with the problem. Since the bully knows they will be protected, their behavior becomes increasingly reckless and hurtful. Continuing this behavior leaves them feeling safe.

The result? Due to your role as peacekeeper, you give your power away, leaving the bully even more powerful. By keeping the peace in these situations, you sacrifice your emotional freedom and right to be respected. Your good intentions enable the abuser.

Considering this, do you realize what high price you are paying for this role? What do you have to give up and ignore to keep the peace within friendships and in the family? Who benefits from your position? I doubt that you are helping in any possible way.

Standing your ground

My clients often shriek when I mention these three words. There is only one reason why people get uncomfortable when I ask, "Why don't you stand your ground?" They answer that it will create confrontation. Sure, it will generate conflict because the abuser knows that by being aggressive and abusive, the other person will back down.

By stepping into the peacekeeping role, the abuser can get away with whatever they want. Again, the peacemaker adopts an enabling role. This situation can rapidly deteriorate to the point where peacemakers become victims.

When faced with the observation that aggressive behavior is unacceptable, anger is a normal response. Yet the reaction of "I did this or that because I was angry" is not a valid reason.

Answering in this way means they cannot take responsibility and control their behavior and emotions. However, this is not your problem! Yet your peacekeeper's role might support the abuser's poor excuse. By being the peacekeeper, you end up taking responsibility for the situation. Unfortunately, your support and validations justify the abuser's unwillingness to own their reaction and take responsibility for their behavior.

Why bother if someone gets angry when you stand your ground? It brings me to the next point. A bully's reaction to your reasonable boundaries is not your problem or responsibility.

The bully has to own their behavior and how they respond. Unfortunately, the abuser might try to dominate and fluster you with their short temper, sledgehammer words, and empty threats. If this happens, take comfort in knowing they are trying to place all the conflict and chaos responsibility on you, and it is not your problem.

Have you ever suggested anger management classes to someone who uses anger to control others? I have! I am not usually the one that handles taking responsibility for another's behavior. On the other hand, if you managed to jump into bed with your best friend's wife or husband, it is fair to say you are part of the anger projected at you.

Why do peacekeepers take on this role?

Peacekeepers actively avoid anger outbursts, and the bully knows this. They know the peacekeeper will step in to save the moment. The wrongdoer feels safe to misbehave because they know someone will take responsibility for their bad behavior. The peacekeeper sacrifices their personal boundaries and right to be respected.

I noticed that peacekeepers have common fears — fear of rejection, confrontation, and abandonment. They also feel rewarded if they sacrifice their truth to keep the peace. For the peacekeeper, peace means safety and peace in their environment, yet it comes at a price.

Unfortunately, the reward that peacekeepers expect is no reward. The more leverage the bully is given through peacekeeping, the more abusive they will get. A good intention driven by subconscious fears quickly becomes a dangerous and threatening pattern.

Confrontation is unpleasant, but ask yourself, "Do I want this pattern to repeat itself for many years to come?" No one likes conflict. However, speak up if someone's behavior is unreasonably manipulative and immorally wrong.

Just because the abuser happens to be your partner does not mean they have permission or any right to behave in an abusive manner. You enable them every time you step aside and let them get away with their behavior. You positively validate their role as the abuser.

In thinking about this, are you an enabler? If you realize that your years of good intentions gave the bully more power, ask yourself, "What stops me from changing this and standing my ground?" Is there a trauma or fear in you that is keeping you from expressing healthy boundaries? Find it, heal it, and reclaim your boundaries.

It leads us to another question: "Is it your job to be the peacekeeper?" I suggest finding another emotionally, spiritually, and mentally healthy, meaningful, and fulfilling job. Find a position that will benefit you.

Love yourself enough to say "no," and express yourself with love and firmness when needed. You can empower yourself calmly and gracefully. When I say this, it does not mean that you should be relaxed and express malicious threats. No, you are still compensating for unresolved anxieties. Instead, believe in yourself, your boundaries, and your right to be respected. If you do not think that you are worthy of respect, you cannot expect others to believe it.

Remember that an aggressive and abusive response is often an attempt to control and disempower a person. Anger is related to feeling disempowered, unheard, out of control, and vulnerable.

Bullies are overcompensating for the lack of control they had in their lives. Instead of enabling them, support them to work through why they are angry and out of control. Remember, it is not your job to fix this. There is a difference between supporting someone and doing it for them.

Chapter 6

Fear that binds us together

Fear is one of the universal emotions that every person experiences. It is a natural and fundamental human feeling. When danger is visible, fear acts as a warning signal. Fear can be caused by both real and perceived circumstances. While fear is a natural reaction, in some situations, it can be more excessive than the actual threat, which can lead to distress and disturbance. Although fear is commonly viewed as a "negative" emotion, it actually plays a vital role in keeping us safe by preparing us to face the potential threat. However, here I want to focus on fears that keep us socially connected. Since we all have common fears, it keeps us connected. We are connected on an emotional, psychological, and social level by our shared fears. When I say this, I mean how we bond because of our collective fears.

When we examine the history of fear, we see it has persisted since the beginning of time. That means the fear of not surviving has been driven by lifelong patterns and continuously evolving and changing in a diverse way. The nature of fear serves one purpose, which is to stay alive. In humans with complex emotional brains, fear has become much more colorful than just being about fear of not surviving. Now, we have fears about almost everything in life. Now, generational fear has also grown out of control and is being passed down from generation to generation. What if a solution to the fear is not given and not passed down? The fear remains, and it continues to stay in the DNA lineage. So, all fears remain in our emotional bodies, but they will remain there and be passed down to future generations unless we break the cycle by healing it ourselves.

Society shapes these fears. Cultures shape it; social circles and family dynamics also shape it. Fears are also controlled and stopped; for example, when a generation takes action, deals with it, and overcomes the fear, it positively affects the DNA lineage. That makes us more resilient to fears. So, you are wondering why some people are resilient and others are not. That is why, with every set of dynamics between people, fear exists, thrives, and continues to grow. It is because our lives are built and designed around fear.

We have to energize fear to stay aware of it continuously and stay connected to it. It is where we lose energy, freedom, happiness, and our quality of life. Some of our strongest bonds with people are based on shared fears. We bond over our fears as we can relate to someone who understands the fear we are experiencing. It feels adequate when we can connect to someone who can relate to us and understand us. Here, we form an instant connection. We are also directly bonded over similar wounds that we share. It creates a connection where there was a disconnection before. It fulfills our deep lack.

It also creates a feeling of belonging. This belonging can be the most vital friendship and hardest one to abandon, significantly when the fear that bonds two individuals together change for one of them. When it happens, there is a 50% chance that we could feel incompatible. We might not always be aware of it straight away.

We could think that something is different, something is off, or just not quite the way it used to be. So, the frequency alignment between two individuals is shifted.

We always grow, heal and change, and so other people also grow, heal and change. However, people who have bonded with us do not always heal with us or at the same pace. So, we can feel significantly weighed down by our inability to express our past fears. We most likely sabotage our progress and healing journey as we fear being isolated and alone. We also have a fear of rejecting others and being rejected. So, we continue to play small in our life. It is because if we were to supersede someone else's wound, we would make them feel inadequate. However, we would make them think something is wrong because they are not moving to the next stage or place with us.

When we move to this level of change, we can feel even more fear in the person we are bonding with, as they could feel that we are changing. However, subconsciously, they need us to stay the way we are so they can relate to and feel connected to us. Thus, the more there is disconnection, the more we will act unknowingly to stimulate the fear of change. People fear letting go of the familiar fear itself. They might subconsciously protect us hoping that we do not change because they are emotionally invested in us living with specific fears. It is what binds us to them and them to us. Some people emotionally invest in us, so they need us to stay as we are. It is because if we change, then we destabilize the foundation.

We destabilize the foundation upon which their perceived security is based. We also find protection in people to whom we can relate because we feel connected when we can relate to someone. We feel like we are part of a community, which automatically creates a feeling of acceptance and togetherness. It is what we all subconsciously want. When we feel accepted, we feel less defective. When we are not accepted, we feel something is wrong with us. No one sees our value and our worth. It is not an empowering feeling.

A powerful example is when we look at two people who are overweight, both have insecurities that the other can understand. Perhaps they feel vulnerable because they cannot shake off the extra weight. Both of them know they look more or less the same in size. So, there is a bond already, by the instant acceptance of one another. This acceptance creates a feeling of belonging. They know their partner will not reject them because of their weight. When one of them loses weight, they inspire or trigger the other partner.

In most cases, it triggers them because of the changes in the other partner, who now loses weight, causing the other one, who does not want to lose weight, to feel even more inadequate. It is because the person they could relate to is now changing. They are transforming into someone with different beliefs and values around health, so they feel disconnected from them. The one losing weight brings up the other partner's resistance to the underlying causes of their excess weight and the fear of change. Here, the fear of change is generally related to the fear of coping with change. So, when we live in fear, we learn to cope with it and build our lifestyle and relationship dynamics around it. That is why healing and letting go of fears is so hard. Since it means change, it means a change in a significant and impactful way. It will have a powerful effect on every aspect of our life. So how to make the change graceful, and how to recognize it?

Step One

Accept change. Change is part of life. However, we dislike change because we do not have control over how specific changes played out in our life in the past. Therefore, we need to consciously decide that we are, from now on, in control of ongoing changes in our life.

Step Two

Recognize whether we have people in our lives who give us space to change, or do they change their attitude towards us when we are changing something about ourselves or our life that would not be affecting them. However, they somehow make us feel that our change is affecting them. It is essential to recognize whether we have healthy support. Clear communication can do wonders at this moment, especially if people in our life are not supportive. If that is the case, explain and communicate what support we need. Do this with ease and grace. It is because how we deliver our message could significantly impact its outcome. Sometimes we must communicate what we need. That is why we must understand and start trying to share what we need, even with our close people.

Step Three

We need to develop a strong relationship with ourselves. The stronger we are connected to our sense of self, the more confident we will feel. We will feel less inclined to sacrifice our identity and also our growth for the sake of acceptance. If we have changed ourselves so much to be accepted by a partner, then we need to ask ourselves, what is the partner emotionally giving us which we cannot feel on our own? What made it worth it at the time to change your identity?

Step Four

So, when you look at the above question, how can you give that emotional experience to yourself without relying on someone outside of you? The answer to this question is your ticket to emotional freedom and away from fear-based bonding.

Chapter 7

Dealing with a controlling partner

Freedom is an integral part of social life and one of people's most basic needs. Human development incorporates increasing human capabilities, which are necessary for freedom. Human development is the most significant aspect of enhancing the quality of life, and freedom is a crucial means of achieving this goal.

Everyone needs to feel that they are in control of their lives. It is our natural desire to have control over our lives. It conveys a sense of security, harmony, and safety. However, what happens if this control and freedom go into someone else's hands? What happens when someone's need to control others becomes so intense that it violates the rights or well-being of others? People start feeling burdened and frustrated in their life if someone tries to control them excessively.

Practicing control encourages actions that can enhance general well-being. As with many other human characteristics, control comes in various forms and can move into a toxic zone from general well-being. A "controlling personality" is influenced by a need for protection. Almost all controlling actions are motivated by fear, such as the fear of being abandoned, being poor, or being alone. Even if the desire for control is not conscious, fear can make a person want to control the situation of the people around them much more.

We may meet controlling people in many parts of our lives. They are everywhere. We see them at work and social gatherings, and they are in our family and our relationships. Controlling people can have a much more significant impact than they should, especially if the controlling person is our partner. It is acceptable to have some control conundrum, but it becomes a problem when it starts to influence our quality of life. It is essential to understand their intentions, to know how and when to respond to a controlling person.

Why do people become controlling?

Controlling people often overcompensate for their lack of control during their childhood. They are desperate for love, affection, and nurturing. The most critical need they are trying to fulfil is to feel safe and sure of what they have. Also, controlling people have been abandoned in some way, often in a traumatic way that changed their life. Being overly controlling is their way of preventing themselves from getting hurt again. Their instinctive need to be in control overrides logic, and it often stems from a deep fear of being alone.

The more control the abuser has, the safer they feel. Being in control of people and their circumstances gives them false security and self-reassurance. It creates the illusion that nobody will abandon, hurt, or control them. The intensity of the abuser's controlling need relates to the lack of control they had during their childhood.

Exploring this person's childhood relationship with their parents can be helpful. A great deal of a controlling person's unresolved issues they have had with their mother or father will most likely be projected onto a partner. Sounds familiar? Maybe you resonate with this, or maybe you don't.

You can change and put a stop to sabotaging patterns

Being strong and empowered to walk away from circumstances and people that constantly challenge you and whose intentions and actions sabotage your progress can be a daunting thought. It is especially true if you rely on them for some support in your life. Creating necessary changes in your life that would support your goals and self-worth is often a big challenge for people who find themselves stuck with a controlling partner.

Usually, controlling people do not want to change their behavior patterns, as it serves them in one way or another. If you find yourself moving away from someone who does not give you the emotional freedom to grow, then you have to ask yourself if this is what you want for your future.

Remember, as you move forward in your own life, you are not responsible for saving or helping people who do not want to be supported (in this case, it might be the controlling partner).

It will help if you recognize that you are attracting controlling people. Controlling people might meet an emotionally unfulfilled need within you that is, in this case, emotionally and mentally unhealthy for you. However, because we fear we might not meet someone else who can meet our emotional needs in a certain way, we often hold on to outdated relationships and people we have outgrown.

When you heal this part in yourself, your attraction to controlling people will subside. Controlling people meet your need and association which you made with a controlling parent. You feel familiar with controlling circumstances, even though it might be emotionally and mentally harmful and can suppress you.

Always ensure that you are working through your stuff, as this places you in a stronger position to attract someone who will meet your needs in healthy ways. Need is never a healthy basis for a relationship as it only creates more lack in your life. The more you need someone to complete and fulfill you, the more likely you will settle for less than what you deserve.

When considering someone with control issues, ask this question: "What is this person's quality of life?" The happier controlling people are, the less they will feel the need to be in control of you specifically. When controlling, people are happy and content; they feel safe and in control and will feel less inclined to be overly controlling.

Moreover, they easily give others emotional and physical freedom when happy. The depressed and unhappy controlling person, on the other hand, will have a forceful need to be in control.

One can ask whether this person always felt the need to control social gatherings, be in charge of others, and attend to the needs of others before looking after their own needs. Does this person give other people a reasonable level of freedom to make mistakes and love them simultaneously?

It is essential to realize that being controlling does not necessarily mean that someone is abusive. Being controlling can also mean ignoring your own needs to meet the needs of others. People neglect their need to focus on others because others rely on them. The more control they have over others, the more important, valued, and safe they feel.

This example again boils down to feel safe. This example shows that what seems to be good intentions can be controlling issues subtly projected onto others.

People that had controlling parents or role models can have control issues themselves. As a child, you rely on your parents for guidance. When a child sees their parents acting in a controlling and aggressive manner because of challenging circumstances, the child will most likely adopt this behavior (not in all cases).

At some point in their lives, the child will realize that to be safe, survive and cope with challenges, they must behave the same way as their parents did in order to overcome their challenges.

When parents control the child's environment by being overly controlling, you should explore why the parents have these control issues in the first place. Are they overcompensating for the lack of control they had during their childhood? The more consistent the message from the parent, the more the child will follow in the same footsteps.

Children follow in their parent's footsteps because it makes them feel safe. Children see and learn the necessary "tools" to cope with challenging situations and become overly controlling. Remember, this is the only example thus far in the child's life; they have seen no other way of life. The underlying basis of these situations is that the child copies and applies patterns observed during childhood. The child's life and environment reinforce issues that existed long before they were born.

There are examples of people with control issues, even though their parents were not controlling. These individuals may have had a challenging time at school. Even though they had wonderful parents, safety and protection from their parents were lacking during school hours.

The result is that they might have felt unsafe, insecure, and stressed. The only way the child copes with stress is by becoming possessive of belongings, clinging to something that makes them feel safe.

This situation can escalate into control issues by compensating for the lack of protection, safety, and control experienced during school hours. They transitioned from an environment where they felt in control to one where they felt out of control. As a result, the child felt highly distressed, scared, and out of control. It is one example of why we could encounter control issues.

There is often an unspoken rule in relationships that a partner automatically has the right to abuse and control the other if given the opportunity. It is an old school and disempowering belief. No one has the right to control or abuse you just because you are in a relationship and there is a power game at play. You should never ignore this type of behavior. If you ignore it, you are enabling the controller or abuser, validating their power game, and the problem will escalate.

Are you familiar with the sayings, "Oh, let's just sweep that one under the rug," "Let it go; you know what they are like," or "You have to do that." My response? "No, I do not have to do anything that I do not want to do." You are well within your right to say "no." There may be times when it is better to compromise, as long as you never feel resentful, submissive, trapped, or enraged when you compromise. Any of these reactions is a sign to look deeper within—it means something is not quite right.

Where do you draw the line with a controlling partner? When are you entitled to say no? When controlling behavior becomes dominant in a relationship, the relationship becomes a burden. So, it is essential to draw boundaries if your partner excessively controls you.

You should draw the line when you feel upset, restricted, trapped, or controlled by your partner. For instance, you should draw a line if your partners take your things away from you as punishment. The angrier you feel, the more disempowered you will feel. You will also feel disconnected from your partner.

Consider why you are feeling upset or trapped. What about this situation removes your freedom of choice or ability to feel free? Is this situation triggering an unpleasant childhood memory? These questions are essential, as they will give you a better understanding of your reactions and why they are triggered.

This understanding makes it easier to handle a controlling partner. It all contributes to empowerment, and you are more powerful when you come from a place of empowerment rather than anger.

Do you need to be accepted by a controlling partner? Is their acceptance so vital that you are willing to lower your worthiness? Is it essential to find out why you think a controlling partner needs to accept you? Is your controlling partner triggering rejection wounds from your childhood?

In my opinion, you always have the right to say "no" and to express boundaries with your controlling partner.

I have told several controlling people, "Just because you are in a relationship does not mean that you can treat them in an abusive and controlling way." "You do not have the right to control your partners."

We tend to make things hard for ourselves, especially if we suffer from low self-esteem. We always seem to think; we need this person; we need this, or we need that to compensate for our own emotional inadequacy.

Sometimes you might find yourself in a situation where you rely on your partner for support. Of course, that is fine, but sometimes things can get a bit complicated. Boundaries are unclear, and we get taken advantage of, especially when we need support, as we feel in debt to our partner helping us.

It results in poor personal boundaries, and we second-guess our entitlement when it comes to saying no, especially when there is a demand for our time and energy. Avoiding full dependence on a partner can greatly improve your self-esteem and confidence. Otherwise, you will feel that all your power is in someone else's hands.

If a partner is supporting you, always make sure that you know their boundaries. Likewise, they should know your boundaries for different circumstances. How will you exchange this? The clearer you and your partner are about what is acceptable, the easier it will be for you to find common ground.

It also helps you to avoid being taken advantage of, as your partner will have the upper hand, possibly playing power games back and forth. Either way, you feel controlled as you find yourself in a position where you feel less powerful and worthy of speaking up. Know that some partners are not willing to find that common ground. The reason for this may be their rigidity and stubbornness.

Remember that, in most cases, it is not your fault that a partner may be controlling, stubborn, or rigid. They, therefore, have no right to project controlling patterns onto you. I have told this to several controlling people; the expression on their faces was priceless.

The more you need something, the more you will attract the concept of "lack" into your life. Have you noticed that the more you complain about something, the more you attract that very thing you are complaining about? That is how powerful you are. Now, imagine what would happen if you changed that complaint into an empowering positive affirmation and repeated that affirmation as many times as you complained.

I believe in self-empowerment. Self-empowerment is also necessary for relationships. I think I am empowered enough to choose how I want to be treated by my partner. I love myself enough to take action against controlling people, regardless of how much I love them. I choose to be around a partner that respects and loves me regardless of my race, culture, and beliefs. I decided to have a partner who communicates with me and treats me in a way that builds my confidence.

Like many of you, I have had my fair share of controlling treatment from a partner. It is not acceptable. We are well within our rights to speak up and express our self-worth. Standing up for ourselves does not mean that we have to confront others; confrontation should always be our last resort. Instead, we can set boundaries in a loving yet firm way. We can even practice saying "no" in ways that will not lead to confrontation.

Setting boundaries is important in any relationship. The best way to express ourselves to someone is by starting the sentence: "I feel........ when you do........" By always starting our sentences with "I feel," no one will be able to deny our feelings, even if they refuse their actions.

Always express how the actions of the other person affected you. Never explicitly blame them because if you do, it will provoke confrontation. Through blame, we will create a situation where the abuser feels attacked, and a defense will surely follow.

In practicing saying no, resolve the trauma from your past that made you feel guilty when you said no or set boundaries. There is no reason to feel guilty. Guilt stems from a childhood where you were made to feel guilty for doing or saying something. Move away from this and create a life with relationships that work for you.

Chapter 8

Dealing with a narcissist

We live in a world where narcissism is rising. We may not realize it, but we frequently interact with narcissistic people. I believe there is nothing more destructive and dangerous for us than being in a relationship with a narcissist. It is a psychologically, emotionally, and physically unpleasant and abusive experience. A relationship with a narcissist is full of misrepresentations, deception, and dishonesty. It is an experience that no one deserves to have. There are several clear signs we should watch out for in a partner that suggest we might be dating a narcissist. If our partner is one, maintaining the relationship will be difficult. You might feel you are diagonally parked in a parallel universe. However, maintaining a relationship with a narcissist is not impossible.

Sometimes it is the right thing to fight for our partner, and sometimes it is best to leave. Though, when we invest time and effort into a relationship, leaving it is not easy. It is even more challenging to deal with a them or those with an inflated sense of entitlement. They fabricate information to keep us interested while constantly destroying our self-worth. However, before we label a person as a narcissist, we have to see narcissism from a broader perspective. Moreover, we must be aware of the essential narcissistic traits to stay in a safe zone.

We may be inclined to label an individual as a narcissist, which would be incorrect in every respect. This individual may be egotistical or self-centered, but that does not make them a narcissist. A person who lacks empathy and has an overwhelming demand for attention is the true definition of a narcissist. Therefore, someone who shares photos on WhatsApp or Instagram stories does not meet the criteria to be identified with a narcissistic personality disorder.

Defining a Narcissist

To be a narcissist, a person must have a narcissistic personality disorder or NPD. These individuals share the following characteristics:

- A strong feeling of superiority.
- The persistent need for acknowledgement.
- They know so little about other people that they could be considered quite self-centered.
- Lack of empathy for others.
- Maintaining relationships is difficult for them.

Dr. Fran Walfish, a relationship psychotherapist, classified NPD as a spectrum disorder. Another American counsellor, Rebecca Weiler, classified narcissistic individuals as overly self-centered individuals who cannot feel empathy. NPD is a psychological illness, and like other psychological illnesses, it lacks a clear borderline.

Source of Narcissism

Although the origins of narcissism are not fully known, some childhood traumas and events are known to contribute to NPD development. Here are a few examples of these events:

- Abuse in all its dimensions, including physical, emotional, and psychological torture.
- A startling incident.
- The absence of parental or guardian supervision.
- Receiving a lot of attention from parents or other relatives.
- Excessive expectations.
- Unhealthy and unfavorable criticism directed towards or from family members.
- The parents' unnecessary attention to physical appearances.
- A lack of self-esteem.

The Criteria for Diagnosis

The American Psychiatric Diagnostic and Statistical Manual of Mental Disorders created a 9-point diagnosis criterion. As a result, this criterion received the designation "the 9-pointer," and in compliance with it, people must possess the following nine characteristics to be classified as a narcissist.

- A heroic sense of self-worth or self-devotion.

- Obsession with fantasies of great beauty, love, strength, and success.
- Inordinate desire for admiration.
- Strong entitlement desires.
- They think they are special and can only find pleasure with unique people.
- Excessive abuse or exploitation of other people.
- Lacking any empathy.
- A fallacious assumption that others are envious of them and so being resentful of others.
- Acting as though they are superior to others without justification.

To be a narcissist, one does not necessarily need to possess all nine traits. They need to have five of the above nine qualities. The most narcissistic features are the hardest to recognize; if you are close to the individual, it is even more challenging. Only a licensed psychologist can diagnose them.

Traits of a narcissist

Although the requirements appear to be very straightforward to comprehend, many things might be going on in a narcissist's mentality that we cannot comprehend. In order to better understand this, let's break it down even more.

The need to have an epic sense of self-love or self-importance

It is an accurate description of a narcissist. We sometimes misunderstand that a lack of compassion is due to an exaggerated sense of self-worth. However, this inflated sense of self-worth is much more prevalent than anything else. A narcissist genuinely thinks they are extraordinary with a God complex.

They can only interact with renowned or extraordinary people because they think they are better than everyone else. Through this idea, they develop a strong sense of self-worth and assume they deserve special treatment from others. Sometimes, they embellish or even lie about their accomplishments to get additional attention.

The need to live in a fantasy world

Since they have a strong sense of self-importance, their perceptions and opinions about themselves are irrational. That is why they live in an imaginary world. They frequently experience remarkable success, love, and all other great things in their imaginary world.

They cling to this imaginary world to escape their inabilities. They immediately disregard any evidence that contradicts their mindset. No matter how hard you try, they will not come out of their imaginary castles. If they feel intimidated by your opinions, they will become enraged quickly, and the situation may deteriorate.

The excessive need for admiration

Narcissists require constant admiration to fill them up like a large empty tank, yet they are never full for some reason. They surround themselves with individuals who continuously admire them. They cannot live with only one or two compliments. They need to have their egos nourished regularly.

That is why any relationship with a narcissist becomes prejudiced. Since they already have a relationship with themselves, it is not a good relationship. The only reason they keep a partner is to have someone to shower them with compliments every day.

Additionally, when their partners cannot soothe their egos, they will turn to psychological and emotional abuse to get what they want.

The excessive need for entitlement

As we have already noted, narcissists think they are more remarkable than everyone else. It makes them believe that they are destined for special treatment everywhere, and they genuinely think this. They believe that they should get anything they want without being questioned.

Since they feel that everyone else is there to fulfill their demands instantly, their feeling of superiority has no limitations. They dislike being ignored; therefore, they will get hostile or even violent if you do not fulfil their demands.

The need to exploit people

Narcissists are not compassionate. They are unable to recognize the needs and emotions of those around them. They see humans as products. This absence of empathy leads to a lack of remorse. They feel no guilt for their misdeeds. That is why they do not stop to consider their actions before taking advantage of someone. They do not do this to hurt people; they do not understand how others feel. They are unable to comprehend how their actions affect those around them. Therefore, attempting to make them understand your emotions will not be helpful to you. They only see themselves and their feelings.

The need to be arrogant

When it comes to keeping up a perfect image, narcissists are very weak. They will become hostile if they notice anything you own, but they do not. They will feel threatened by you, if you are more loved, renowned, affluent, or have more friends.

They will see this as a challenge and will make it their mission to degrade you whenever they have the chance. They will still harm you even if you pose no genuine danger to them. They believe this is the only way to preserve their ego.

They can attack you in a variety of ways. They can purposefully criticize your accomplishments. They can utterly disregard you or begin to abuse you by talking negatively to you and can even spread misinformation about you.

How to know if you are dating a narcissist?

Almost all of us have been somehow accused of engaging in a few of the behaviors mentioned earlier. So, by this point, you must be wondering whether you are dating a narcissist. It will not be easy to spot narcissists because they are very good at manipulating people.

Consider the following signs to gain a better understanding of your situation:

They shower you with love at the start

At the beginning of a relationship, they will shower you with love. They will complement you excessively, making you feel out of this world. They might even say they are madly in love with you. They will stay in touch constantly, so it becomes easy for you to fall for them.

Kaleidoscope Counselling is a non-profit organization that aims to provide counseling to anyone older than twelve years. Nedra Glover Tawwab, the founder, defines a narcissist as someone who legitimately feels more exceptional than everyone else. As we have already observed, this belief encourages them to believe they should only be surrounded by extraordinary people.

Moreover, once you decline to do whatever they ask for, you will notice a significant change in their personality. That is why you should be careful if you feel someone is coming on too strong at the start of a relationship. If an inner voice within you keeps telling you, it is too early for anyone to fall in love with you since they might not even be sure of who you are, believe it!

It is always about them

They enjoy embellishing their accomplishments, stories, and other aspects of their lives. They engage in this behavior to feel superior to others. It is time to go if you sense that your partner is more interested in their accomplishments than yours and seems uninterested in what you do. However, you must pay close attention to their pattern to realize this. What happens when you begin to talk about yourself? Do they feel confident in your achievements? Do they inquire about your day, or do they only speak of themselves?

They are always on the hunt for a compliment

Even though this might not necessarily be a narcissist's characteristic, it is something to be mindful of. Some individuals lack sufficient self-esteem; therefore, they seek lovely compliments from their loved ones.

Narcissist partners will appear to be self-confident, but if you do not soothe their ego with compliments, they will scheme ways to hurt you.

Additionally, Shirin Peykar, LMFT, supports this statement. Genuinely self-confident individuals do not require constant praise and attention from others. This quality is only apparent in every narcissist.

They lack empathy

You might be dating a narcissist if you do not feel heard or seen in your relationship. NPD patients lack empathy and cannot comprehend that other individuals have emotions. It is why they cannot understand the concept of caring for others.

They only care about themselves. They are, therefore, the least concerned about your issues. You may begin to feel unworthy when you are in a relationship with someone like that. They will not be conscious of the emotional or physiological trauma they cause you. At the beginning of your relationship, you might be able to ignore your partner's inability, but it can become a significant issue for you as time goes on.

You must constantly remind yourself that narcissists are not interested in dating. They merely need a puppet who will follow them everywhere. They only need someone who always flatters them and gets everything they want. They will not value you until you start to feed their ego. Once you stop doing it, everything will go wrong.

They pick on you constantly

If a narcissist can inflict harm on others, be mindful that they will also target you. They will initially do this as a prank to see how you respond, but it will soon become a habit. They will constantly tease and be cruel to you because of your actions. They express this behavior because they find it unacceptable to witness others succeeding in life.

They will try to destroy your self-worth, since that is the only way to prevent you from discovering how strong you are. You must leave this situation and consider: Does your partner acknowledge your achievements? Do you notice a change in their behavior every time you succeed? Do they give you the impression that your achievement is not your own and that you only succeeded because you had someone's support?

They are constantly gaslighting you

Not only are narcissists excellent at lying, but they are also skilled at manipulating circumstances to make you feel like you are insane. They will do whatever it takes to control the situation so that they can present you as the villain.

Here is how to recognize a gaslighting situation.

- Your anxiety is increasing and significantly worse than before you started dating them.
- You constantly reflect on your behaviour.
- You are always totally accountable for anything that goes wrong.
- You have a persistent feeling that something is wrong, but you cannot identify it.
- If you are too sensitive, you always find an excuse.

They never apologize

They will never apologize, since it is always your fault when something goes wrong. Fighting with them is pointless because you will eventually have to apologize, even if you are right. Looking for an apology is like looking for a steak in a dog kennel. They barely acknowledge their point of view when there is disagreement. They do not see a problem with what it is. They observe how it impacts their reputation and themselves.

So, do you feel unheard? As if it does not matter what you think? Do you frequently feel guilt for things that were not your fault in the first place? It is time to ask yourself a question: Can your partner compromise?

Is it possible for a narcissist to change?

What can you do to support your partner at this point? Is being a narcissist a lifelong condition, or is there anything that might assist them in getting through its difficulties?

A narcissist can indeed improve and change over time. However, it takes a lot of effort and determination to change. No matter what you do, nothing will help your partner unless they are determined to improve.

The author of Disarming the Narcissist, Wendy Behary, demonstrated that narcissists are not hopeless cases. If they put a lot of effort into their personality, they can learn empathy. Empathy will activate all of their emotions once they encounter the worst feelings, they have hidden inside of them, and their personalities will change. Therefore, only a narcissist is aware of what must be done to transform oneself truly. Getting medical and emotional support is essential to the success of this personality change.

Is a narcissist capable of love?

You frequently question whether a narcissist truly loves you while you are in a relationship with them. The only explanation is that since narcissists can only wholly love themselves, they cannot truly love anyone unless they undergo personal change.

They view everything as a game and ignore other people's happiness. So, their affection for you will not last over six months or a year. After that, it is all about themselves. If you marry them, they will not understand your demands as a partner. They cannot love you until they change. They can change only on their own and without assistance from anybody else.

Is narcissism curable?

For NPD, there is no treatment. However, there is still hope, as many treatments are being tested, and narcissism research is constantly being conducted. Emotional therapy is an integral part of the treatment of narcissists.

The main issue preventing this therapy from being successful is that narcissists do not acknowledge that they are defective. They are ideal for them. They think they are superior to everyone else. How can you heal someone who cannot analyze the situation?

Mental health treatment is the only form of treatment currently available. To benefit from this treatment, narcissists must acknowledge that they have a problem and require assistance.

Read between the lines

If you date a narcissist, it will be a lot of fun at first, but then you will have the worst nightmare of your life. All of this elegance and appreciation is the beginning. It is only a fantasy that might harm your mental health if you believe it.

The following are some steps you can take to interpret these words correctly and escape the web they have trapped you in:

See them for what they are

They will first make you feel fantastic. They will give you their undivided attention, make every effort to work with you, and give you the impression that you have discovered your soul mate. However, it is crucial to step back and observe what is happening. Please do not defend their actions, and do not feel that your sensitivity is excessive. Don't ruin your dignity!

Do not give them the authority to mislead you.

Establish boundaries

A narcissist is incapable of recognizing a boundary because they do not view you as a person. They do not acknowledge your emotions since they only want to utilize you for their gain. That is why they will not respect any boundaries you establish.

They have a strong sense of entitlement. Because of your affection for them, you could even be willing to endure their unacceptable behavior. However, it will only harm your emotional and physical health.

That is why it is necessary to establish boundaries. When you feel uncomfortable doing something, speak up and take a stand. The narcissist will test your limits and attempt to undermine you, but never forget that you need to stay strong.

Ways to help deal with a narcissist

To some degree, we all exhibit narcissistic qualities. You meet the definition of a narcissist when these characteristics are so ingrained in your psyche that they dominate all you do.

In actuality, these narcissists do not feel good about themselves subconsciously. They are in pain constantly because they believe they are powerless to do anything. However, when dealing with a narcissistic personality, you should know the following:

Understand their position

Having a broader perspective could be beneficial. Try to comprehend what people think and feel and understand their points of view. Take a deep breath and imagine they are powerless when you grow tired of hearing them talk about themselves all the time. It is the only thing they are capable of doing. Without realizing what they are doing, they carry it out. They consider it as something normal.

Stick with your boundaries

Maintaining your boundaries is essential for keeping your emotional health. Choose your conflicts wisely; you do not always have to be available to let them scream and shout at you. If you have to, make up an excuse. When dealing with a narcissist, it is essential to keep a balance.

Avoid being toxic

They are toxic, and they believe you are toxic as well. Prove them wrong by not being toxic at all costs. Although it will be difficult, remember that the main aim is to avoid competing with them in this game.

Understand the difference between kindness and empathy

Remember that it is not your responsibility to heal them. In this area, there is nothing you can do to help them. All you can do is to be nice. Trying to help or tell them about their narcissistic traits will only worsen things. They will begin gaslighting you, which could be catastrophic.

How to limit a narcissist

You can decrease your interactions with narcissists and maintain a healthy personality by employing the following strategies:

- You should spend less time with them. Try to stay away from them. It is best to see them as little as possible.
- Discuss your feelings. Even if they do not listen or act uninterested, expressing your emotions will relieve some pressure on your shoulders.
- With them, do not rush into anything. It will be challenging because narcissists are charming at first but do not reveal everything to them. Maintain a safe distance.

Paying no heed to a narcissist

The best thing you can do when dealing with a narcissist is to ignore them. In the long term, this may be advantageous since they will start to feel as though they no longer have authority over you. It may cause individuals to reflect on their behavior and consider whether their approach to using others is appropriate.

You must make an effort to indicate that you are uninterested. It may cause them to turn their focus away from you. You are not responsible for this person's well-being, so keep your distance.

Conclusion

If you believe you are dealing with a narcissist, you must speak with a licensed mental health professional. It can be your partner or a member of your family. You cannot handle the situation independently since you lack the necessary information.

Understand that it is always acceptable to step away if you can no longer handle it. You do not have to do anything for anyone, and your mental and physical health should come first.

Identifying Gaslighters

Over the past few years, gaslighting has become a more prevalent subject as more young people openly discuss mental health. There are frequent reports of emotional abuse, including gaslighting. Overall, that is positive since it can help us avoid stressful and toxic relationships by raising awareness of this type of emotional abuse.

Gaslighters usually want to control the other person by misusing reality and making them doubt their thoughts and feelings. Gaslighting is also known as emotional manipulation. Emotional manipulation is common in unhealthy and toxic relationships and has much in common with other forms of physical and emotional abuse.

Although it can happen in family or workplace interactions, gaslighting is most frequently seen in romantic relationships. However, it is essential to understand what gaslighting means and how to spot its apparent indicators in a relationship before we can accuse someone of practicing it. Let's look more closely at the meaning of "gaslighting," its effects on mental health, and how to recognize this behavior.

It is psychological harassment in which the they try to control the other person by planting doubt and uncertainty in their thoughts. They manipulate reality to make their victims question their principles, convictions, perceptions, and even conceptions of reality to exert control and authority over them.

In the play "Gaslight", the affluent author Patrick Hamilton explained this psychological suffering exceptionally well. The play's debut performance took place in London in 1938, and the reviews were excellent. Names like Noel Coward and King George VI were among its admirers. The drama was adapted into a movie in 1940, and when it caught the attention of the Hollywood media in 1944, they used it as the basis for a film starring Ingrid Bergman. When the play Gaslight was written, individuals hardly ever discussed psychological disorders, let alone acknowledged the marital problems brought on by precarious mental health.

The performance begins with the famous couple, Jack and Bella, in the spotlight. Jack is perplexed in that he fluctuates between being friendly, compassionate, and frigid. Bella is cautious around him due to his uncertainty. When Bella complains about Jack's behavior, he begins to orchestrate events so that she begins to doubt her sanity. Jack also has a history of flirting with women outside of his marriage.

He visits the upper floor of the house and purposely leaves the lights on while hiding her things there. The lights in the lower part started to fade as a result. According to psychological abuse, it is an accurate depiction of gaslighting. Today, "gaslighting" describes a particular form of psychological abuse where a person begins to doubt their sanity. In reality, they are not the primary problem.

Numerous initiatives have been launched to raise awareness and help people understand gaslighting. In 2018, Oxford Dictionaries named "Gaslight" as the word of the year. The American Dialect Society named "Gaslight" the most practical word of 2016 in its annual report. In the UK, coercive control laws were created, making it illegal to gaslight someone while they are in a close relationship.

Gaslighting has also been portrayed in a lot of dramas and movies. For instance, a narcissistic gaslighter controls heroin in the movie "The Invisible Man." He misleads her into thinking that she is insane, which is the epitome of what it feels like to live with them.

People are now expressing their doubts about anyone who exhibits gaslighting characteristics. For instance, a Love Island contestant, Adam Collard, was charged with gaslighting by Women's Aid.

Why is gaslighting so prevalent? What devious force is responsible for it? Kate Abramson, a philosophy professor at the University of Indiana, describes it as the "deepest form of moral wrongdoing."

Think about how it would feel to experience the worst and then learn that it never happened or was imagined. Now picture having suspicions about your partner cheating or lying. You can see their habits and everything they do that point to cheating and lying, yet they claim you are being paranoid or controlled to draw attention away from their behavior. They will argue that "partners continuously flinging themselves on them" justifies their behavior. It causes you to doubt your convictions.

In addition, Kate Abramson claims that the denial of it as it is happening is just as problematic as the abuse. Telling the victim that their response, rather than the deed, was wrong invalidates their point of view. The victim can no longer challenge the actions once they doubt their judgment. Kate is confident that everyone understands what is right and wrong. This definition is picked up by gaslighting, which prevents us from interacting. It is highly unsettling.

Domestic abuse is more frequently committed by using gaslighting. For instance, the artist "Freya" was severely gaslighted and coerced by her ex-husband. He began by isolating her rather than physically abusing her to crush her spirit, claiming that the artist's friends always reach her husband. After that, he forbade her from working. Whenever she sat down to paint, someone would tell her that she was neglecting the kids or their marriage.

He left her so puzzled that she could not distinguish between right and wrong. She no longer trusted anyone. He constantly told her that she was ignorant and foolish. He was so cunning that he was even manipulating their young children. He would explain that since their mother cannot console them, only daddy can do so.

After isolating her effectively, he began hiding her belongings. She would have her belongings with her one moment and lose them the next. She is confident that she placed her wedding ring on her microwave before it quickly vanished. She remembers her husband being especially happy that weekend, and she knew she would be in big trouble if she did not get her engagement rings in time. She became upset and sought to cover her hands before he directly asked her what was wrong.

She specifically denied losing anything when he expressly inquired whether she had. He dragged her downstairs and opened a rarely used cabinet, revealing Freya's misplaced rings inside a champagne glass. Following this finding, the ex-husband yelled at Freya a lot, frequently calling her a failure and a liar.

The practice of gaslighting is not limited to our houses. In addition, it occurs at work. Our coworkers are capable of gaslighting us as well. They might undermine our work, disseminate inaccurate information, or even mock our concepts.

As a result, we start to question what they are. Where and how do they pick up this nasty trait, exactly? There is no way to know for sure. They could have had a very challenging upbringing, or they copied this behavior even from simple observation.

They might have had a small-scale success with it once, encouraging them to persevere until they centered their entire identity around it. In the book The Gaslight Effect, Dr. Robin Stern discusses this and claims that gaslighting is not always intentional. She said, "It might be that you've learnt that shattering someone's alternative perspective is a method of putting yourself in confidence when you're feeling unstable."

Women have comprised the majority of gaslighting victims. According to a UK study, men used coercive and controlling tactics far more frequently than women did. However, this does not exclude the existence of females. In her book, Dr. Robin Stern claims to have treated numerous men who had fallen victim to gaslighting by other women, particularly young girls.

The victim is bullied by alleged friends, who tell her she is oversensitive every time she objects, the same as in Rachel Simmons' book Odd Girl Out. Gaslighting can quickly develop into a dangerous trend.

This individual, according to Abramson, is someone unable to accept another person's point of view. They perceive the opposing viewpoints as threats and use this as justification to eliminate the opposite view and its origin. To protect your sanity, Sarkis suggests staying as far away from them as possible.

Identifying a them

Divide and rule

Splitting is the most typical characteristic of them. By disseminating lies and promoting false information, they enjoy dividing people. People turn against one another. For instance, they might accuse you of something seriously wrong that a friend allegedly said about you, while the friend may have said nothing.

Manipulative apologies

The phrase "I'm sorry if you feel that way" is not a genuine apology, even if they continue to express regret. An authentic apology involves accepting accountability for one's conduct rather than attempting to influence how you feel. They cannot apologize in person and will only pretend to be sorry to gain what they want from you.

They love to butter

As long as they get what they want from you, they will praise and flatter you nonstop. Once they succeed, their true selves emerge, and they lose interest.

They are spectators

They enjoy watching a fight or a dispute that they instigate. They use deception to mislead people, which occasionally results in a conflict between two parties. What will they do? They will observe and be delighted with the results.

Chapter 9

Anger in relationships

The most common reason for why partners sabotage their relationships is unresolved anger and resentment. Often, people will subconsciously behave in ways that push their partner away as a way to punish them for past hurts. There can be many other reasons for why partners might sabotage their relationships, such as feeling unworthy of love or fear of abandonment, but unresolved anger and resentment is by far the most common.

If you find yourself repeatedly getting into arguments with your partner or feeling like you're always on the verge of a break-up, it's likely that you're subconsciously sabotaging your relationship. If you can't seem to let go of the anger and resentment you feel towards your partner, it's important to seek professional help so that you can resolve these issues and save your relationship.

If you're not sure whether or not you're subconsciously sabotaging your relationship, here are some common signs to look out for:

1. You constantly criticize your partner
    Do you find yourself nitpicking everything your partner does? Do you feel like you're always on their case, even

when they haven't done anything wrong? If so, it's likely that you're subconsciously trying to sabotage your relationship.

2. You withhold affection

   Do you ever find yourself withholding affection from your partner as a way to punish them? Do you feel like they don't deserve your love and attention? If so, this is a huge red flag that you're sabotaging your relationship.

3. You withdraw emotionally

   Do you ever find yourself withdrawing emotionally from your partner? Do you shut down and refuse to communicate when things get tough? If so, this is a major sign that you're subconsciously sabotaging your relationship.

4. You have an affair

   Do you find yourself attracted to other people, even though you're in a committed relationship? Do you feel like your partner isn't enough for you? If so, it's likely that you're subconsciously trying to sabotage your relationship by having an affair.

5. You constantly argue with your partner

   Do you find yourself arguing with your partner all the time, even over trivial things? Do you feel like you're always on the verge of a break-up? If so, it's likely that you're subconsciously sabotaging your relationship.

Understanding Anger in Relationships

Getting to know anger

In life, we go through a lot of experiences. We go through several emotional, psychological, and physical experiences. Our emotions significantly affect how we react to certain experiences and feelings in specific circumstances. We have a variety of emotions, for example, happiness, sadness, fear, and anger. However, I would like to explore anger, which is a powerful emotion. Let's start by defining anger. Anger is an immediate, natural reaction to threats. Many things trigger the emotion of anger.

So, I want to talk about anger from a large perspective. In this part, I will particularly focus on the root causes responsible for triggering the emotion of anger in us. It is because the definition of anger alone is not enough for us to understand this powerful emotion, and so we have to dive deep into its root causes from where it emerges. I will explain the causes of anger in detail, which will help you see anger from a more in-depth perspective.

Anger is a feeling and an expression that you all have felt. However, you probably do not know why you feel angry sometimes, so you do not see what triggers this emotion. Anger is not necessarily a bad reaction. How far you take it and what you associate with it can either make or break your experiences. It is essential to truly understand the problem itself when you tackle any problem that you are facing. What is the problem? Why is it there? Why do you feel you have lost control over it?

We all feel we have lost control over a problem because it is still a problem. For example, you might be on the receiving end of anger, but you might not always know why someone is reacting the way they do. The worst thing is that we mostly do not know what to do about it. So, we are going to explore anger from many angles. We will deeply analyze its root causes, secondary gains, and hidden benefits. We will also look at when it is constructive or destructive because anger is a powerful reaction. This reaction can also help you to achieve specific results. Still, if anger is not used correctly, it can leave behind a trail of consequences such as emotional, physical, and even spiritual damage to you or someone else, especially in relationships.

During my research, I learned that anger is not an emotion. For example, when working with someone on their anger issues, I always ask, "How did you feel just before you felt angry?" In most cases, when I get deeper into the trigger, they usually say before they felt the anger, I hear them saying either powerless, helpless, or out of control.

Anger is also a symptom of our emotional reactions. It surfaces when we cannot suppress and hold certain emotions, cumbering us. Anger is also an instinctive response, driven by the reptilian brain rather than the limbic system. I will share my personal experience here as an example. During my teenage years, my anger consumed me so much. I felt so powerless towards past incidents that I overcompensated by using anger to reclaim my confidence and sense of power.

However, I did not realize then that I came from a place of fear and vulnerability. I built a false sense of confidence around my anger. I was not a happy person back then. I felt like a victim, so I used anger to feel strong and demand respect. With these patterns, I achieved the success I wanted in my early twenties. However, consequently, I was so alone, unhappy, and depressed. Nothing in my life was fulfilling enough to make me happy.

My anger resulted from overcompensating for the challenges I experienced as a child. It was also a behavior that I copied from authority figures, especially my father. I eventually felt like I had a right to reclaim the power I thought I had lost. However, it was just suppressed by the intense thoughts that I had. Deep down, I had no confidence in myself, felt vulnerable, and did not know what my boundaries and limits were.

Anger comes forward when a person is also very controlled and suppressed during childhood, which I also experienced. Then, this threshold for controlling and suppressing circumstances becomes overly sensitive. Your capacity to fight, ignore, and reject it becomes so incredibly oversensitive that someone or circumstances can easily trigger these old wounds from the past.

Anger can come forward because of trying to regain control of circumstances that we perceive we have lost control of. Anger can also be an inherited pattern from your parents. So, ultimately, anger is a symptom of a much deeper root cause.

I always refer to anger as a symptom of another emotion. It is almost like a secondary emotional reaction. The reason I say this is that there are always deep-rooted emotions beneath the anger. It is crucial because certain emotions were felt over a while or within a few minutes that became so strong that the body did not know how to resolve or express them emotionally. It caused the body and the mind to feel disempowered, unsafe, and vulnerable.

If your body perceives a threat, whether an emotional threat or a threat that could lead to your death, it will react as though it has now been challenged beyond the threshold point where the body feels safe. Now, this threshold point, in this case, also means your ability to cope with a particular behavior or reaction from someone or your environment. Once this threshold in your body has been reached, you are bound to have a reaction, which is anger, in most cases. Anger is the result of the fight instinct. How you express this fighting instinct would depend on various circumstances and the level of threat you are experiencing. The more a situation or a person is triggering an unresolved emotional wound from past trauma, conscious or subconscious, the more extreme your reaction could be.

Let's look at different types of emotional triggers you can have before we get to the expression of anger. First, we have a conscious wound trigger. What does it mean? Let me clear it up with an example. Suppose you had a partner who you feel lied to you about their whereabouts. One day you were so angry because it reminded you of when your ex-partner lied to you about their whereabouts, and you found out that they were cheating on you. At that moment, when someone lies to you, it triggers your deep, unresolved wound of infidelity, betrayal, and loss of trust.

Then we have a subconscious wound trigger, which happens when something in your environment triggers your anger. At that moment, when you react, you are only aware of the anger you feel, and you are not necessarily consciously able to connect to why you feel upset and angry. For example, you might feel outraged when someone moves into your lane, cutting you off while driving. We all have experienced this level of frustration on the road. Now, apart from feeling angry, you might also feel disrespected. You might feel that your territory has been taken over by someone else, so you feel completely disregarded and not valued at that moment. You might not be able to make a conscious connection to the deeper root cause of why you are angry, apart from just that the person cut you off, and you are really upset.

Here, I am talking about the deeper root cause of your anger because there can be plausible reasons behind your anger. However, you are not consciously aware of it. We are looking at moments from your past that could trigger it. These moments can be associated with feeling disrespected, disregarded, unworthy, and feeling your territory has been taken over or controlled by someone. It is an example where you do not immediately make that conscious connection as to why you feel that level of rage. It just exasperates you. However, it is because of deep implicit memories that we do not necessarily have conscious awareness of.

On the other hand, the subconscious mind knows they are there, and your environment, relationships, dynamics, and anything can trigger these implicit memories to flare up. So, you feel the memories emotionally, but you do not cognitively make the connection and put the memory together with the emotion you are feeling. What you are feeling is the biochemical reaction, meaning the emotional reaction to that. In this way, your subconscious mind triggers more challenges because you do not clearly understand the root causes. It leaves you even more upsest off because you can feel these emotions so intensely, but you can't trace them back. What makes it even more frustrating is that it is hard to find a solution to resolve the anger you feel because you do not necessarily know the root cause. Whereas with the conscious trigger, you know the root cause, and you can take active steps to resolve that old trauma.

I want to split anger into two more categories. The first category is symptomatic emotional reactions, and the other is a very primal, primitive reaction that is like an instinctive reaction. Let's look at what anger is used for in these examples. Here, we will focus on the emotional survival of human nature.

Anger is used to regain control of the situation you usually feel you have lost control of and the situation when you feel highly unsafe. You also use anger to defend yourself to either emotionally or physically protect yourself. We can also use it to indirectly demand respect from a person we feel disrespected by. Or to feel and to be heard. It could also be to establish an emotional boundary. Anger is used to get something done faster, even to intimidate people before they intimidate you, and to release intense built-up emotions. Moreover, you may use anger when you feel unworthy and shameful to protect and express yourself with more confidence emotionally.

Now let's look at the instinct of survival strategies of anger. Anger or the fight instinct is used to protect you from a perceived threat. Perhaps someone or something is challenging your ability to feel safe. It may be challenging for you to express a boundary between yourself and someone. Also, remember that we have emotional and physical boundaries. Let's focus on the physical boundaries, such as your personal space around you, which could be your home or your garden when you go to the gym or put your stuff into a locker. It is like saying, "Do not touch my stuff," which clarifies your personal space and physical boundary.

We also use this instinctive anger to defend what we perceive as being our possessions and as stopping someone from taking them. For example, to be very competitive to secure our financial stability which will lead to our survival and safety. Moreover, you use instinctive anger to ensure you and your family are safe, like when you defend a child or a partner's safety. It is our tribal instinctive response combined with a fight instinct. This survival instinct can be so strong that it overrides common logic.

You can also use anger to act on your subconscious desire to maintain your standard of living. So, there is a significant ground to cover when it comes to understanding the root causes of anger.

So, there is your crash course in anger. In the next few sections, we are going to dive deeper in order to understand anger in the context of relationships.

Anger identity

Anger is a natural and common emotion we all experience at some point in life. Most people always associate anger with something negative. However, anger is sometimes necessary for our survival and emotional, mental, and physical safety. It is acceptable to become angry if someone is teasing you unnecessarily. In this way, you are trying to protect yourself and create your safe space by using anger. What makes anger worse is its inappropriate and excessive use for innocent people.

When we revert to anger to get through life, then anger can quickly become part of our identity. People will always refer to you as an angry person. However, we need to realize that there might be some deep-rooted causes of this anger. It's not an excuse but applying emotional intelligence here work wonders.

How do you know your anger has become your identity? It is a great question because, just like with anything else in life, when we do something so much on such a large scale, it can feel like it is a part of us.

However, anger has become a part of our experience, but not necessarily a part of our identity because, deep down, we are designed to be calm and peaceful. But then life happens and our environment shapes how we feel. It changes how we react, and how we react becomes an aspect and a part of our character. Trauma might become part of our character and personality because it shapes us. However, how we deal with that trauma can tremendously impact who we become as a person.

Let's look at how our identity is formed around anger. In this case, it is important to remember that the body is biologically programmed to look for stress, threats, and anything that could be a threat. We are naturally very pessimistic, at least our ancestors were, and we are breaking the cycle and shaking off these habits.

This natural part of our body is always aware of potential threats.

When you look at biology and how the body reacts, anger can feel that it is becoming a part of you, which it is not. It's a coping mechanism of the body. If we don't manage these responses with care, then how it is expressed can alter your quality of life and shape your identity around these responses. In this case, I am referring to anger.

In reality, anger is a part of your experiences because your life experiences and environment trigger anger. If the triggers are not there, you are relatively balanced.

We are an easygoing species, and we are designed to be very harmonious. If we were designed to deal with so much stress and anger, we would not have all these psychological problems and stress-related physical ailments related to stress.

When you also look at this aspect of anger being an identity, it could be because you identify so much with anger. After all, it gives you an identity. Therefore, your dominant emotions can become your identity.

Suppose you are constantly in an angry state where you feel under stress and have to defend and protect yourself. It surfaces as fight and flight. Anger often relates to unresolved threatening emotions, like feeling unsafe, threatened, and vulnerable. When we feel vulnerable, our rational mind is not a match for the body's fight-or-flight response because our instinctive responses are automatic.

In addition, the psychological aspect comes with the physical aspect. So, when you are in that state of distress, your brain becomes deprived of blood and oxygen, and now these resources rush directly to your large muscles. It is because we have this urge to move fast. It is also why when someone is dealing with a lot of anger and stress; it can reflect in their work and success. Now, this can be helpful if someone is good at sports or taking part in very high-risk activities.

We often see people who carry a great deal of anger with them, yet they are tremendously successful or at least excelling in one area of their life. Often, anger is used to propel a person forward and toward their desired goals. Anger is not just associated with our identity, but also with accomplishment, success, and so forth. It was the case for me. I wrote all about it in Abundance Mindset.

However, deep down, when we look at the accumulation of what created the identity, it is unresolved trauma. How we cope with trauma is what shapes our identity. Most people use anger to keep themselves safe and as a way to cope with their past.

Anger is not your identity when you feel angry. Anger is an experience that you are having. Acknowledge the difference between your identity and anger.

This acknowledgment will help you detach yourself from the perceived concept and the illusion that you are anger.

Misdirected anger

Everyone gets angry at some point or another. It is normal and healthy to feel this way. However, it is crucial to understand how to control your anger and where to direct it. What happens when anger goes to the wrong person or thing? This type of anger is known as "misdirected anger." It emerges when you direct your negative emotions toward someone who is not the genuine source of your unpleasant emotion.

While most people have experienced misdirected anger, it is important to identify its recurring patterns. If you take your anger out on the wrong person or situation, you are not alone. This type of anger outlash is more common than you might believe.

However, it is important to learn how to deal with anger effectively. So, it is essential to ensure that anger is directed at the appropriate person and level to be expressed and resolved effectively. It is because, in countless cases, misdirected anger has destroyed relationships, opportunities, and lives.

Let's explore this topic in detail, focusing on the root causes of misdirected anger. We cannot find a solution for misdirected anger if we do not see its root causes and how it happens. So, misdirected anger is when you consciously or subconsciously take out build-up emotions in the form of anger and rage on someone who triggered you. In this case, your action was unfair and out of alignment with the situation at hand. There are so many examples of misdirected anger that I will share with you. Rage and anger have many root causes. However, anger and rage also share a commonality. The final outburst of anger is your subconscious emotional body showing you that you have hit your threshold and your ability to suppress old wounds, relating to feelings of powerlessness, unsafe, and feeling out of control.

No peace has ever been found through anger, emotional destruction, or war. So, what worked for me was to think at the moment of anger, what is the best thing about my current situation? This approach worked really well for me. It might not be for you, but it's worth trying.

When you are angry, you might have noticed that all you can focus on is your emotions' rage and the intensity of it. It drastically narrows your capacity to see an immediate solution that could be right in front of you. Instead, you look for ways to defend yourself after the argument, which takes your focus away from the core reason you are in such an explosive situation in the first place.

Most of the time, when a person has an anger outburst, it has different underlying triggers and hidden wounds. For example, what are the triggers in the moment of an immediate argument? At the moment of an argument, think about what is the best thing about your current situation. I call this "break state" meaning, you think of something completely the opposite. Why? This thought immediately shifts your focus to a more positive outlook. Why is this important? Because in a more positive outlook, you can be more solution orientated rather than being part of the problem.

In this case, when I say the best thing about this argument, it sounds funny, but let's take it one step further.

Let me use an example here to answer this question. I was fighting with a friend, and we had a big disagreement about meeting at a certain place at a certain time. She was late, and I was on time. I am always on time. Time is very important to me, and I value my time and other people's time. However, my friend shares a different value regarding time. My friend also did not know that in the past, my dad would physically punish me when I was not on time.

So, when my friend was late, I exploded when she arrived. I took my anger out on her, explaining how she disrespected my time and did not care that I had to wait for her. However, when I paused at that moment and asked myself, "What is the best thing about the situation?" an interesting and unexpected answer came up. The answer was that I could establish my worth by being treated with respect and dignity. It was a subconscious expression of my need to feel respected by my father and not by her.

My anger outburst towards my friend was a suppressed fear of feeling powerless towards my father, and then the loss of control I had when he physically beat me up. So, what I realized in that moment of anger was that I was fighting for respect. I was fighting for respect from my friend. However, she was not the root cause of my intense, angry reaction. My reaction was intense and disproportionate compared to how small the issue was. So, you see, in most cases, anger outbursts are misdirected attention that has been building up from the past. Was she wrong for being late? Absolutely yes, but my reaction towards her was out of context.

Let's look at another example. My dad always told me I could do nothing right. Everything I did was always wrong. I was always criticized because of this. I sabotaged many projects and goals because my father's voice was always on my mind. My dad would always say, "You cannot do it. You are not smart enough. You will always fail. Are you stupid?" I know my dad was a special person and I don't mean that in a positive light. However, because of these lingering voices of my dad, I always repeated these toxic thoughts. I tackled every project with this type of mindset.

In most cases, I would never complete a project. It was not because I did not want to, but because I did not want to prove my dad right by potentially failing. So, quitting and giving up was easier than facing the possibility of failing.

When I finally got a professional job, I did not have a choice just to quit my projects. I was obligated to complete it. It was an intense internal emotional fight, and it brought up fears about failing and looking stupid in the eyes of my managers. So, one day I was at work, and a lady called me about a project that I had completed, and she was shouting at me, saying that I had made a mistake and messed up the project. She just hung up the phone, and the anger in me exploded.

After the phone call, I looked at the project again and realized that she had made a mistake in her analysis when she checked it. The office that I worked in had two buildings. A street separated one building, and here I was. I got up from my desk and I marched. I did not walk; I marched across the street, walked into the other building, into that woman's office, and took out all my anger on her. That entire floor went quiet. I shouted and explained to her that she needed to get her facts straight before behaving the way she did.

The human resources manager came into her office to see what was happening. I was so lost in my anger that I did not care about any consequences at that moment. Thank goodness, there were no consequences for me. However, I learned that the woman I was shouting at had the exact same pattern with other people. So, HR saw this. I did not realize it, and everyone just overlooked what happened. My point here is that her reaction was not polite. It does not matter what her history is, but my reaction to her was completely out of line as well. But did she ever cross my path again? Hell no, and that suited me perfectly well. When one wounded person triggers another wounded person you are sure to have an unpleasant argument.

However, I realized my anger was there because of the injustice I felt towards my father, who always pointed out my mistakes. This woman triggered the old memories, and that wounded part of me. She tried to open up a case against me. HR just laughed, and they told her it was one of many cases against her. She had no right to claim because this showed her what it felt like to be at the receiving end of anger. So, she eventually agreed, and we both learned a lot from that experience afterward. I also asked myself, "What was the best thing about that moment?" I will not back down when faced with false accusations, but I could have done it better.

So, the next time you feel an angry outburst surfacing, immediately assess your situation because the circumstances are triggering the root causes of your anger outbursts. There may be a possibility of a wounded part of you now trying to come to the surface so that you can deal with it. In a moment of anger, before you react, ask yourself, "What is the best thing about this exact moment?" It is because a deep subconscious part of you is trying to take advantage of a situation to release suppressed emotions you cannot suppress anymore.

Ask yourself, "What is this moment giving me a chance to release right now? How can I release this constructively without hurting someone? Whom am I really furious with?" You might be surprised by the answers that come forward. However, either way, you will have much more clarity behind your anger and the real reason you feel anger. Instead of feeling powerless against anger, you can take constructive steps towards unraveling the real triggers of your anger.

Victim of anger

What if your partner brings anger problems into your relationship? What if you are the one struggling with anger in relationships? What if you are the victim of anger? Where do you draw the line, and how do you handle it? In this case, you need to see the deep-rooted causes of anger that might result from an old and unresolved trauma of your partner. Let's look at some helpful insights in this regard.

The reason why a person brings their unresolved anger into a relationship, consciously or subconsciously projects it onto the other partner, could be that they feel safe enough with that person to show them their wounded side, but also in a guarded way by masking it with their anger. It is like someone is asking for help and support. It is like someone saying, "Please help me, but do not come too close."

Anger is not an excuse for being on the receiving end of someone else's anger because that anger is, most of the time, not the other person's fault, and can be completely unrelated to them. For example, if you are at the receiving end of it, you might hold a safe space for them to offload how they feel. However, in most cases, their anger is not actually about you; it is more about how they feel deep down. Their anger is a very complex expression of unresolved wounds from the past. It could have been triggered by the environment or a simple conversation with you that brought up strong conscious or subconscious wounded memories of their unresolved past. Their anger is now being taken out on you. So, anger is also used in relationships to control a person emotionally.

The reason why this level of control is there could be because of many different reasons. It could be due to fear of losing you, or maybe they think you will leave them. So, they might push you away before you hurt them. It is a classic example of rejection and abandonment trauma that is now projected onto a person in a relationship. It is often the most challenging type of dynamic to deal with because it requires self-improvement for the person challenged with anger to resolve this wound and stop this cycle of projection.

It is not your responsibility if you have a partner with anger problems. It sounds harsh, but you cannot heal on behalf of someone else. They must be willing to heal this themselves. So, right now, you might wonder, where does that leave you? The answer is simpler than what we tend to make it. It is because, in most cases, we are so attached to believing that someone can change that we start to make excuses for them. We also strongly believe that someone can change and will then be able to meet our unmet needs. We think they will meet it if we stick to this relationship and support them in some way. Then you stick around, and the person does not change, and you still stay there, hoping that this person will change until the relationship's pain and burden become so heavy that you suffer.

It is at this stage when a relationship can either make or break you, meaning either leave for the sake of your well-being and come to a conscious understanding of why you stayed so long in that relationship or stay and continue your path as it is.

It begs the question, if you stayed too long or are still in one, then do you need to be needed by this person? Did they not give you a sense of value at the time and you continue to search for it? If so, it begs the important question, "What do you feel was missing in you emotionally that caused you to feel so distracted by this relationship? Was anger a part of your childhood experiences?" It means maybe your parents were angry people so that anger could have become your comfort default position. Being around angry people felt normal.

I notice that people who grew up in a very angry and aggressive environment set the platform for anger to become their comfort zone. It becomes normal, and they subconsciously seek partners and circumstances similar to their childhood environment. So, sometimes their need for love and acceptance was sometimes met by abuse and anger. It begs another significant question, "Was this maybe the case for you?" It is because when this pattern is repeated enough, a person can subconsciously start to associate love with anger, and then they become a frequency match.

It is like a feeling that makes someone attracted to people who have abusive tendencies and anger problems. Then your common logic kicks in after a while by responding in a negative emotional state, realizing that it is hurting you. However, your delayed reaction towards these negative circumstances shows that even though it feels normal, it is not healthy for you.

Leaving this environment is most likely the best option if the other person is unwilling to work on and resolve their anger. If your partner does not resolve their anger and does not want to improve themselves, staying with them becomes a conscious choice. Being unhappy is a conscious decision, especially when you know the person will not change.

Now, another angle on this topic of dealing with an angry partner is the copycat approach. In this approach, someone can also use anger to control and intimidate you. The reason for this could be that they observed their parents or a person they admired having a similar dynamic, so they copied their behavior style and brought it into their relationships. Now they could be using their anger to show that no one can control them in any way, normally due to feeling powerless, suffocated, or overly controlled in their past.

Unfortunately, you are now bearing the brunt and the consequences of someone else's mistakes. In this approach and behavior, it is not your responsibility to fix and tolerate their behavior. Suppose you stay with a partner with anger problems. In that case, it is your conscious choice because the longer you stay and do not take action toward working through these challenges, the more acceptable this pattern and cycle become until it becomes the relationship dynamic.

Accepting and bringing a person into your life means that there is a part of you that now allows you to be vulnerable enough to love and be loved. It also means that you allowed yourself to trust your judgment, intentions, and the actions of another person. When things in a relationship go wrong, and you felt neglected or abused by the partner's anger, this bond and trust between you becomes challenged.

The cycle of vulnerability escalates because now, not only is your trust in your partner challenged, but it has also disrupted your relationship with yourself because you trusted your judgment to walk into this relationship in the first place.

So, emotional damage is not just done to the relationship, but also your relationship with yourself. Leaving a relationship where the partner is projecting so much anger onto you can leave damage behind if you continue to allow it.

The damage is not just a reflection and a fear of not trusting people. It is more of a question, "Can you trust your judgment again?" Now you know where the biggest wound is lying. Now, the situation where you find yourself can spiral out of control, leaving you with your emotional wounds because sadness and anger have become your shield and coping mechanism.

Here is the second ripple effect of the copycat. It can be passive or aggressive, isolating you from people you meet or being standoffish, irritated, and short-tempered. The list can go on, and you can become angry and sad. It is because these emotions are now symptoms of much deeper emotions that you are currently stuck with.

You can also become stuck with anger and sadness because it is easier to identify and understand these emotions rather than understanding or having an awareness of the deep-seated pain that goes beyond the expression of anger and sadness, which is now being the victim of an angry partner.

It is what I call passing on the torch, but negatively, because the attitude that your partner projected onto you and how you learned to defend and protect yourself against it could become part of your coping mechanism. It will further result in a big chance for you to become the aggressor in future relationship dynamics. If you do not heal the stress of the emotional wounds, you experience in these types of, relationships then it can set forward the path to repeat the cycle.

So do not pass on the torch and do not allow anger to become your new boundary because of what someone else has done to you. It is because most of the time, new people coming into your life are not a part of the problem. They are not responsible for your wounds. It is important to keep it in mind and to have conscious awareness of it so that you can continue to build healthy relationships in your life because you deserve it.

Now let's look at how you can deal with a partner challenging you with anger. So, when a partner loses their patience, what happens? Do you generally overstep and express the boundary they have? Or do you act in a way that is aggressive, and it is out of context with what is taking place in your immediate connection with them at that time? Or do you become the peacekeeper, which only enables them more?

Trying to have a normal and rational conversation with someone angry is futile. The reason is that they are so pumped with adrenaline and their fight-or-flight instinct responses are activated that they are not thinking rationally at the time. So let it go. Let go of trying to have a rational conversation. The best thing to do is to say that you will give them space and you are listening to them.

You do not have to sit there and be blasted with their anger if you feel unsafe, uncomfortable, and disrespected. Listen to these emotional responses because they tell you that your boundaries are now being overstepped, and it is your right to remove yourself from that environment immediately. It is also a moment where you can truly understand your value and self-worth.

Now here, the first step is to become aware of what kind of role you are playing in this. Are you the peacekeeper, or are you the enabler? It is because either way; it empowers the person who is always projecting their anger onto you. Now, trying to minimize any stifle confrontation in your environment is normal. However, when you try to keep the peace and allow the person who is projecting their anger at you to get away with their behavior, you try not to interfere. It's like trying to pet a dog's head that is angry. You will most likely get bitten!

If you become the peacekeeper, then the person with the anger sees it as surrendering. So, when the abuser or the person with anger problems spots your weakness, they think they can get away with their behavior again. This person now knows that your reaction will be the same next time. When it happens again, they blame you for the argument they started or tell you it is your fault.

Violence could even follow, depending on how severe your circumstances are. In this case, you might feel convinced that it is your fault and that you are the origin of the problem, but in reality, you are not. So, here you are, trying to take responsibility for something that is not your fault.

Now let's get to step two. Make a list of words, actions, and emotions that indicate that your boundary regarding how you want to be treated is being disrespected and overstepped. For example, I will go first. I know that my boundaries are being overstepped when I am being screamed at. I hate it when people raise their voices at me. It is extremely disrespectful. I am standing in front of you. Why scream?

So, another warning sign could be to feel unsafe in someone's presence or when you have no free will to make your own decisions.

In this case, now the list can go on. So, your boundaries here are also being overstepped because, in most cases, you do not know your threshold for dealing with an angry partner. It is because by the time you feel hurt or scared or even angry, your threshold and your boundary were overstepped a long time ago, and you are now in damage control mode. You need to act before you reach the point of resentment because, by that time, it is too late.

Now, in step three, consistency is also key. Once you establish your boundaries with your partner, then stick to them. It is because if you are consistent, they will realize that you are serious. However, if you are inconsistent, they will think that you are just bluffing, and they will continue pushing you to your limits.

Now focus on step four. What are you emotionally getting out of this relationship that you won't be able to emotionally feel on your own if you are out of the relationship? Now your mission, if you accept it, is to heal the answer to this question I just asked you because this is where and how people hook into your vulnerability.

Anger and violence

Anger can damage a relationship in a lot of ways. It is often a sign of something deeper and more complicated, and it can also disperse so that both people in a relationship end up angry. After a while, you may not even be able to recognize each other as people anymore, and your basic feelings about yourself may no longer match what you are going through. Instead, you see yourself as an angry, hostile person and your relationship as one in which you are always angry.

The anger cycle changes how we see ourselves, our partners, and the relationship. To change this view and see what is going on, we need to see the deeply hidden root causes that escalate the vicious cycle of anger and violence in relationships. Moreover, we must realize whether we are in a healthy or unhealthy relationship. Remember, we do not always have to be the victim of anger. We can actively stand against this abusive behavior. We have the complete freedom to leave a violent relationship.

However, let's also focus on why we feel trapped and cannot leave an abusive relationship. What makes us stuck in this violent cycle? Surely, it all comes with manipulation, emotional weakness, and fears of rejection and abandonment. Let's see how violence and anger actually play out in our relationships.

I had been in a violent relationship in the past, and I do not take this topic lightly, as I am fully aware of the emotional, spiritual, and psychological consequences of such a destructive dynamic. So, when you are in an unhealthy relationship, you will be exposed to treatment that significantly lowers your reference point for how you expect to be treated. It might be that you have an emotional need that needs to be met. However, with your self-esteem now being compromised in a negative way, you might be emotionally willing to pay any physical or psychological price not to deal with this aspect. It is because of the fear that it will rock the boat in your current dynamics, which means causing maybe more explosive reactions from an abusive partner because you know that if you change, you will go.

Now, this is when you are stuck in a freeze instinctive response, for example, being too scared to do anything to take your power back. When you lack self-esteem because of abuse in the past, then it will be much more challenging to recognize your value, love, and the support you are worthy of in a relationship, yet you do not have access to it. If your needs have been continuously disrespected or your love, for example, was withdrawn from you in a relationship as a punishment for expressing needs that a partner perhaps perceived as being unreasonable, then feeling the right amount of self-worth to express a need will become very challenging over time.

So, your need to meet your needs has been challenged to the point where your expectations have been weakened and lowered for those needs to be met in a healthy way. Moreover, your efforts to meet your needs in a relationship have been rejected or criticized to the point where you kept lowering the bar for this need to be met and for how you would allow yourself to be treated.

It is because you kept adjusting yourself to the reactions of an abuser to keep the peace. Now, unacceptable behavior and responses from a partner have become acceptable because that was the only way to keep things calm and to take the path of least resistance. It is also during this time that you form a dangerous comfort zone. As you start to feel comfortable with feeling uncomfortable, you start to feel safe feeling unsafe.

When you become so used to being abused, abuse becomes normal. It even becomes a lifestyle. Once an abusive relationship ends, you might continue to subconsciously seek out partners that are abusers to reconnect to the old lifestyle that you have become so used to. Despite what the logical mind might think about the situation, physically abusive relationships can be extremely challenging. It is because when your physical body feels threatened as a result of the reaction of a partner, all that you want to feel in that moment is safety.

It is also true for emotional and physical abuse. When you are abused, all you want during that time is psychological and emotional safety, comfort, and an emotional escape from the stress you are experiencing. However, you have no option or emotional resources to support yourself during that time of abuse to relieve you from the psychological stress you are experiencing.

Now, regardless of the nature of the abuse, a similar effect arises where you subconsciously reach out for security. It is what we do when we feel unsafe. However, whether physically or logically, the only person that is there at that moment of abuse is the abuser. Can you see what is already happening here? You see, the abuser is the person who is consistently present in your environment at the time of the emotional and physical abuse. Your need for safety is subconsciously met by the abuser's presence simply by that person just being there at the moment of the abuse.

Here you can see how that cycle and the need for safety start to form, how it is met, and the unhealthy associations formed with your need for safety. It is typical of how Stockholm Syndrome is developed in abusive relationships. It is when, for example, the victim protects the abuser. They stand by the abuser, and they won't leave them. If the cycle of abuse is repeated enough, it can become a lifelong association.

This subconscious pattern makes it so incredibly hard to break the cycle of being attacked and abused. The key to avoiding this is to heal the psychological pain and the trauma that is holding the thought process in place. The neural pathways also formed in the brain of the abusive person are responsible for holding these associations in place. It leads to this toxic cycle of abuse through neurogenesis, which is the development of new neural pathways.

Leveraging this process right now that your brain is now naturally capable of creating new pathways or perhaps neuroplasticity, which is when existing pathways start to heal and change, and they reprogram themselves with new, more positive memories, thought processes and patterns, you want to break that negative cycle.

Remember that abusers get what they want through dominance and creating fear in you. They know they are looking for a partner that is easy to manipulate. They target people who have low self-esteem because it is easier to cross their boundaries and get away with poor behavior. It is also easy for abusers to convince people with low self-esteem that nobody will ever love them as much as the abuser does.

It makes the partner emotionally dependent on the abuser. Their only source of love, which is overcompensation. There is a lack of love. There is a wounded part in this person where they never really had the amount of love they needed. Then the abusers can easily convince their partner that they would be nothing without them. Before the person even realizes what is happening, the abuser has already manipulated them into thinking that he is their beginning and the end.

I also grew up in a harsh and volatile environment, so encountering abusive behavior was nothing unusual for me. It was in the past, yet it felt so familiar. So, if abuse has been a part of your life's foundation, it can be challenging to see your life without it.

People who have suffered abuse also become numb to the harsh reality surrounding them. You can naturally assume that it is also normal because the abuse was normal in your past. You also tend to learn from a very young age to be persistent, struggle against obstacles, and observe how your life evolves. It is because you most likely did not have much choice back then, but now, as an adult, you have.

So, let's explore the warning signs of an abuser.
- Show unhealthy signs of jealousy.
- Do they prevent you from socializing with your friends or try to manipulate your schedule so that you do not have time for your friends anymore?
- Do you feel limited in your freedom when you are with your partner?
- Do they have a short temper?
- Do they also blame you when they can control their emotions?
- Do they have poor self-worth and lack of responsibility?
- Do they have excessive mood swings?
- Are they abusive towards their parents?

If they are abusive toward a guardian, it is a clear sign that you could be at the same receiving end of that kind of treatment because it just shows you how bold they can be.

- Do their parents have a history of drug and alcohol abuse? It is because it can also cause aggression.
- Do they constantly call or message you to check up on you?
- Do they show extreme jealousy when you talk or spend time with other people?
- Do they throw a tantrum or say negative things about people you socialize with?
- Do they call you insulting names in front of others or even in private?
- Are you always making excuses for this person's behavior?
- Do they become overdramatic and have statements such as, "I will kill you if you leave me, or I cannot live without you?"

It is emotional blackmail. What they can also do is deliberately humiliate people and talk down to them.

So, now the question you might be thinking of is, "How do I break my cycle of abuse?" There came a time in my life when I started to notice that something was wrong in my life. It is like that little something in your life that feels out of place and wrong, and you start to look around you to examine your environment and relationships with others. I started comparing my life to other people's lives and relationship dynamics. I started to ask myself, "Why is my life so different?" Why does everyone else not get verbally abused or beaten up?

You look at other people's lives and then realize how utterly unhappy you are with your life because something feels wrong. Then it begs the question, "Why is my life so different?" Someone once asked me, "If you are so unhappy with someone, why do not you leave?" It hit me hard. I was too scared. I had spent such a big part of my life giving my power away to others that I realized I had given up all my goals and dreams for my future to keep the peace. It took that much energy from me, and I could feel how the veil over my eyes started to lift. I realized that I had lost myself to such an extent that I did not even know who I was. I did not even know what my favorite color was. I did not know what I wanted to do with my life. I did not even dare to make my own decisions.

Do you see? So, the path and the healing journey is that you must let go of who you think you are. Your identity is not being a victim. Being a victim is a passing experience. Who you are is so much bigger than that.

Many people who have experienced abuse would identify themselves as victims. Why is this so destructive? It is because your subconscious mind will fight to protect your identity and sense of self. When people see themselves as victims, they overlook the strength and power they actually have within them. People also overlook the fact that they can heal from their past.

To avoid self-sabotage, it is also important to avoid identifying yourself with a harmful and powerless identity. You are not a lifelong victim. You are a survivor and a warrior who can heal. You are the inner resource and the love which was there before the abuse.

Start with the cause of your trauma instead of the symptoms. Feeling like a victim is a symptom. Establish new boundaries and feel worthy. It is important.

It is also finding a balance between your and another person's needs. It is because life is not just about other people and their needs. Life is also about you. It is also about what you want and need. It was also important for me to learn how to ask for support, the support that allowed me to feel safe and in control.

Most importantly, I needed to learn how to ask for the kind of support I needed, not the support that people thought I needed. It is because that is not real support. Real support is people listening to what you need and then helping and supporting you to achieve that.

Remember, if you also have no goal, where is your direction? So, you need a goal. Then, most importantly, you need to release your guilt and shame. It is because how another person treats you and how they act and behave is not your fault. However, they made you believe it was your fault, and you accepted that. No more of that misguided information.

Anger projection in relationships

In relationships, partners become angry sometimes. However, if this anger becomes a routine and a continuous pattern, here the real danger lies. Anger is destructive in such cases, but anger is not always the root pain point. The point is the deep-rooted and hidden causes that trigger anger in a relationship and compel a partner to project anger onto others. In most cases, this deep-rooted hidden cause can be an old unresolved stress or trauma that subconsciously triggers anger. Is it an excuse? No, it means it's a conundrum that needs to be dealt with.

Being in a relationship with someone who has been through a lot of traumas can be challenging if you don't understand their trigger points. But on the other hand, you don't want to feel you are walking on a minefield your entire life. However, we might not always know if our partner experienced a traumatic past. We can observe it when they often act in ways that are hard for us to understand because there might not be a clear reason for an angry reaction. For example, they might quickly get angry, show distrust, have panic attacks, or stop caring you are like, "what just happened?" That is a great question.

First, it is not your job to diagnose a partner, a lot of problems can stem from this. Why? Not accurately understanding the root causes of behavioral problems can cause us applying the wrong "solution" to a problem. I think the outcome is obvious, right?

Trauma can make it hard to process emotions, and people who have been through it often find it hard to explain how they feel. It took me years to figure out my conundrums. It can lead to disagreements and misunderstandings in relationships, and it can be hard for the partner on the receiving end to know what kind of support to give. This is where is where it gets hairy. In my opinion, it's not healthy to try to "fix a partner, because it changes the relationship dynamic from lovers to therapist and client.

The best and shortest answer I can give in a case like this is to go to anger management classes together to support them and you will also learn a hell of a lot. Couples therapy is another option, instead of sending your partner off to therapy on their own. Your way of supporting them could be by doing these activities with them. It takes the sting out of the ego and makes them feel less like they are the problem or "broken" which is not the intention. The reason someone has anger problems is that they don't feel safe in their life. The reason? An unresolved past and a nervous system that is overstimulated because it never regulated itself properly after traumatic events.

Moreover, let's focus on more possible causes and reasons why a partner is projecting anger onto the other partner. In most cases, when anger is projected onto a partner, that anger is coming from somewhere else. It does not just appear on its own. That anger was already present within the person before they entered the relationship. The relationship itself is normally not necessarily the problem, but it can also be what the relationship presents to the person struggling with anger. In other circumstances, a partner or the relationship itself may also serve as a trigger. What it presents is not necessarily the issue here; it is the person's coping mechanisms that are brought into the relationship dynamic that become problematic.

Now, let's split these concepts into three different categories. Category one will be when anger is a part of a person's persona. Then we will look at when anger is triggered by what a relationship presents to a person. Number three, we will examine when anger is triggered by what a partner represents to someone challenged with anger. Ultimately, you will see these three aspects blending in at the end. Yet they also have their importance and meaning. I am splitting this into three categories because we are talking about relationships and not daily life. The primary focus is specifically on when there is much more anger within a relationship than what would be considered normal.

So, let's look at when anger is part of a person's persona. Meaning? It is a part of their coping mechanisms, meaning they use anger to establish a boundary, especially when they feel unheard, invisible, disrespected, embarrassed, or vulnerable. The list can go on. It's not their identity, but rather how they identify with anger in relating to boundaries and protecting themselves when they feel unsafe.

Remember, we all have different trauma points. We all have different ways in which our past has shaped our perspectives and how we perceive people's actions and reactions. So, be mindful not to judge based on how you see it here. You have to step outside of the box with this one.

When the above emotional wounds are triggered, they can trigger anger. Here, it can unleash a fight response. Instead of withdrawing, there is an action that begs the question, "What is this person fighting for?" At that moment, when they feel angry, what are they fighting for? What do they feel has been challenged within them? Normally, deep down, this person feels unsafe. But then it begs another question, "why"? Anger can give a person an adrenaline boosts and also give false power and confidence. This "boost" in energy is what can become destructive if the core wounds driving it are based on unresolved trauma.

What could the potential negative emotions be underneath the anger? Now, we will return to the adrenaline aspect because it is also very important. Here, it can give a person an emotional high in the sense that they feel emotionally and physically confident and stronger in their life. It would then compensate for many negative disempowering feelings they might feel challenged by because of unresolved wounds from their past. So, anyone can trigger them, especially if they are made to feel or to relive certain negative emotions from the past. Their coping mechanism, which is now anger, is triggered to keep them safe and regain some level of control and safety, again, of a situation or person from the past they felt challenged by. In most cases, anger is the final expression of perceived overstepping boundaries.

The person now feels powerless to correct the bridge of their boundaries. So, when anger is expressed, they have reached their threshold and limit of what they can emotionally and even physically handle. What makes dealing with anger challenging is that we do not always recognize when boundaries are being overstepped.

We might not recognize when we overstep someone else's boundaries, because that may not have been the intention. Often, there is no clear sign or communication of these boundaries because the other person might also not recognize it. They only react based on how they feel rather than exploring why they feel the way they do.

Normally, you know you are dealing with an overcompensating reaction when someone reacts angrily with such a volatile response. You are dealing with something deeper here. It is very important to keep this in mind.

So, if anger is a challenge for you and your boundary is overstepped, I am sure you can feel the fire of it. It's more frustrating if you do not recognize it when you feel angry. It is too late. You are in damage control mode.

You can cope with trying to breathe through the anger and fully acknowledge that something is happening that you are not okay with. This fine line can call the shot between a peaceful conversation and a full-blown argument. It is because if you recognize when that line is being crossed before the anger explodes, of course, you will have a much calmer conversation. Unidentified overstepped boundaries here are normally the primary culprit for why people overreact.

Let's now move to category two, when anger is triggered by what a partner represents to someone challenged with anger. Let's consider an example. Suppose a woman is in a relationship with a lot of anger challenges and constantly projecting her anger toward her husband or boyfriend. Here, it could be the partner representing a masculine figure in her life. Perhaps she had a very challenging childhood experience with her father, where he might have abused her, emotionally neglected her, always blamed her, or made her feel wrong for doing certain things. He might have abandoned her or rejected her a lot. These old wounds are now triggered by her partner, who might not have any similarities to her father. He might not even be behaving the way her father did. However, he represents a masculine presence. Her association with men and masculinity is wounded.

What happens is that her RAS, the Reticular Activating System in her subconscious mind, focuses exactly on aspects that resonate with how she feels in her environment and the RAS will disregard everything else. So, whenever she sees her boyfriend or her husband (who represents the masculine) negative memories come up. She feels tense and unsettled around her partner.

In her subconscious mind, her partner still represents a masculine figure. Now the RAA will filter and look for different mechanisms in this person or ways that he behaves and words that he might use. In the slightest moment, it can catch something that she would relate to as being abusive or a wound from her past. So, here the connections have developed. The trigger in her is reinforced, and it becomes stronger. She unintentionally filters in aspects of her father. Even though her partner might differ completely from her father, the slightest thing can trigger her. So now, subconsciously, she is looking for mistakes, flaws, and faults in her partner that could strike as a similarity between the partner and the father.

Now, the sad part about this is that she only focuses on potentially threatening behavior that could come from her partner because that is what she is emotionally filtering in. She looks for signs of abandonment, rejection, abuse, and neglect. Her intention in looking for these signs is to seek safety. It is a very strong subconscious safety mechanism and destructive cycle. It is because now, the boyfriend or the husband, who is innocent, is paying the emotional price for something that her father did in the past.

She subconsciously might also punish her partner for presenting this masculine figure in her life. In hindsight, who she is punishing is her father, and her partner is just an innocent puppet in this case. The partner with the anger challenges also takes the anger out on the other partner because they finally feel safe in that person's space to let go of the anger, to let it explode.

Unfortunately, it comes out in a very abusive or punishing way sometimes, but it does not intend directly to cause harm to the partner. The motivator behind the anger is some unresolved pain from the past.

Now let's focus on category three. When anger is triggered in a relationship by what the relationship presents to the person, this is quite common, and I see this happening often. We all have different definitions of what relationships are and what they are based on, especially because of our experiences with relationships and how we observed our mother and father interact with each other. It can also be how we perceive family dynamics, relationships, and all these experiences. It shapes our definition and experiences that we have had within relationships, bringing together the conclusion of how we feel about relationships and what it presents to us.

Here, I am referring to a relationship that this person found themselves in, which is also in the past. It could have made them feel confined or suffocated like they had lost their freedom. They could have experienced a lot of abuse, not just from the partner, but maybe the partner had family members or friends who were not necessarily as kind to the other partner. When you look at a relationship, it is not just about the partner. It is about their friends and family as well. It is the entire package. It becomes a relationship dynamic and does not just include singularly the two partners. What creates conflict here is that we look for love, comfort, and nurturing in relationships. We all do that to have our needs met.

Now, wanting to be in a relationship dynamic is very normal. It is our biological and emotional need. However, if you have trauma and stress associated with being in a relationship, you feel bound, trapped, and conflicted. It is almost like you want it, but you also fear it simultaneously. So, now you can relate to certain aspects of this. It is because we all have had some bad experiences with relationships. However, it is normal to learn from experiences. It is also normal to feel the way we do in bad relationships.

There is an aspect where we remember what it felt like so that we can avoid repeating them. However, sometimes the memories of these negative experiences can be strong and destructive. The way that we go about trying to avoid living these memories can become even more destructive. So even though a person has, for example, stepped into a relationship, the relationship dynamic can trigger older memories in the person from their past, such as feeling suffocated or trapped.

These negative emotions triggered by being in a relationship will most likely trigger old coping mechanisms. It causes our body to feel like it is reliving the past, and we might start behaving in ways we did in the past to keep ourselves safe. Even though the relationship itself might be beautiful, the slightest trigger can open up enormous emotional wounds, setting us back into a painful cycle. So, here we project all our past coping mechanisms into our new environment that are not aligned with our experiences.

This situation creates the biggest conflict. However, the distress we are feeling can often be so great that we struggle to control our reactions. It is because we ultimately want to feel comfortable and safe, and our mind and body perceive themselves to be in a past event. Our body will react and try to regain control of its perceived out-of-control circumstances by reverting to the fight-or-flight instinct reaction.

Now, when you look at anger challenges regarding anger within a relationship dynamic with a particular focus on these three points, they are quite fundamental and very important to explore. You can also see how these three points can exist separately, but ultimately, they are also blending together into one challenging and problematic situation.

So, be mindful and look at what can be beneath the surface. It is because, in most cases, when you look at a volatile reaction, it is an absolute indicator that something deeper is going on.

Violence and anger in relationships

Healthy and loving relationships are one of the most valuable blessings for us. It makes us feel safe, happy, and comfortable, and it makes us feel complete. We have an emotionally, mentally, and physically healthy life if we have healthy relationships, especially a loving and caring partner. However, what if this beautiful bond and sense of safety, comfort, and happiness turn into stress, fear, rejection, humiliation, intimidation, and emotional manipulation? What if you get a violent and abusive partner instead of a loving and caring one?

Surely it is going to be a traumatic and stressful experience. However, it is also important to understand that anger and violence are not always necessarily intentional actions. Is it acceptable? Absolutely not.!

We all have some elements and the same emotional traumas and triggers for our angry reactions. Different scenarios can cause us to become violent. Violence does not just have one main cause, which is trauma associated with feeling unsafe. Violent anger can also be learned behavior.

In most cases, anger is caused by feeling unsafe. Feeling unsafe stems from a loss of power and control. No one enjoys feeling unresourceful! I dive deep into these topics in my book Reclaiming Your Inner Light.

So, if you know someone who is very violent, then these insights will be very helpful for you. Or, if you are the one who is challenged with violent outbursts, then you might find some key insights here that can help you to understand certain motivators that could be driving these outbursts. You will also find tools and strategies to resolve the old wounds behind this type of behavior.

Let's first look at the addiction part of violence in relationships before jumping into potential root causes. Here I am referring to emotional addiction in this case. So, when you hear the word addiction, it is normal to think it must be a substance addiction. Substance addiction is like when we make a perceived positive association with something destructive to our emotional, mental, and physical well-being. However, with violence, the addiction can be, for example, with the adrenaline rush of lashing out. It can also be the emotional reward of establishing psychological and physical safety, dominance, and control, indirectly leading a person to feel safe again.

Now that you have this bit of background information, let's explore different scenarios that could underlie causes of a person becoming violent. Let's look at jealousy, the need to dominate, and the lack of emotional connection. When you look at this, you look at a person who had an upbringing in their childhood where there was not a lot of physical safe contact or emotional and physical connection. There was lack of eye contact. If eye contact had been made, it could have been made in a very aggressive, demeaning, and threatening way. These aspects are crucial to developing healthily over time because it helps the Hippocampus, the emotional brain, to develop in a healthy way, allowing a person to bond in a safe way. I know more brain regions play a role, but here, my focus is on the Hippocampus for this argument. It's our long-term memory.

Thus, the more stimulation the Hippocampus can have with these safe interactions, the more a person will be open to communicating, talking, touching, touching, and having eye contact, as communicating in a graceful way. Most importantly, they will feel safe to connect with others. Any abuse that took place in a person's life had a tremendous impact on the development of the hippocampus, nervous system and amygdala (our panic button). So, what happens is that the more under-stimulated the hippocampus is, the more dominant the primitive part of the body will be, which is the instinctive response. If a person was raised in an unsafe environment, their instinctive responses would be a lot more in control than their emotional brain. It is because, normally, our emotional brain and the frontal cortex are more in control of our day-to-day activities, like how we act and react.

In this case, in the reptilian mind, instinctive responses will dominate. It is where we have an instinctive fight-or-flight response. So, if they were exposed to a lot of aggression and violence or were physically abused, look at which part of the brain is being triggered the most because physical abuse makes you feel unsafe. You feel unsafe because there is a physical attack on the body. You feel threatened, and so you react. In this case, their reaction could have been the opposite, maybe to hide, freeze or to feel numb.

As they mature, anything can trigger this subconscious memory of feeling unsafe and threatened. They could react and overcompensate for what they could not compensate for as a child. If someone becomes violent, that is a good example of where they overcompensate. So, there is also another scenario with that. When you look at parts where this person also feels that he has to fight for what he wants, he has to fight for his truth and to be understood. He has to fight for respect because that happened in their childhood.

These childlike coping mechanisms are now being carried over into their adult life. However, the coping mechanisms and the subconscious memories have not healed and transformed in order for communication between brain regions such as frontal cortex, hippocampus and amygdala, has developed.

Consciously, they know they should not behave in these destructive ways. When push comes to shove, they do that because the primitive actions and reactions along with coping mechanisms, are much more dominant.

Let's also have a look at scenario two. Perhaps there were moments where violence and anger were used as a way of expression because communication was not practiced, or communication was expressed through violence. These moments can be, for example, when our parents communicated to express a boundary to correct us or to do something that would make a point. If they wanted to carry over a point, they used physical violence. Look what is happening, "that is how I communicate. That is how I get my point across. If I feel unheard and disrespected, I need to carry over that message physically." So, violence can also be a person's way of communicating. It is not right. However, here we are just explaining and exploring certain aspects of their communication.

Let's look at trauma and wounds associated with being communicated to. Anger is the symptom, and the root cause is a lot of pain and wounds behind this communication. Violence and anger were also used in this case. It is used to communicate, to gain control of a situation that causes a person to feel out of control, driven by their fear of losing control of a personal situation. Their way of gaining control again is to act violently and to intimidate. So, the moment when they feel powerless, humiliated, stupid, or embarrassed in a conversation, there is most likely going to be a very volatile reaction. It is why violence can also gain control of a situation in a toxic way because the ramifications cause more harm and trauma to people affected.

So, let's have a look at scenario three. Look at what made me feel safe in the past that now causes me to feel unsafe, powerless, and to lose control. It is super important. Let me explain because this example will bring me to the next part of this discussion: associations.

When I say what made me feel safe, it is what actually made me feel unsafe. For example, when you look at a person's childhood, you realize that a parent is meant to make a child feel safe. The parents are his source of protection, safety, and love. However, if this parent were violent, this scenario would destroy the child's concept of what is safe and what is not. This child's need for safety is met by violence and feeling unsafe. These people can feel safe feeling unsafe.

When a child needs to feel safe or comfortable, and that need, whether expressed verbally or physically or not even expressed at all, is just a desire. Then to be met with an act of violence anchors in a negative and toxic association with safety and comfort. It is important because, as this child matures, its subconscious mind will remember this association. When they find themselves where they need to feel safe and comfortable, they react violent in order to feel safe again. Violence is the tool they use to reach a state of safety.

However, how can an association be formed here? So, when you feel a need for safety, your subconscious mind will look for older memories formed when you needed to feel safe. Your subconscious mind will then remember the violent acts against you, creating a biochemical reaction in your body, preparing you for an actual attack. It ultimately heightens your fight-or-flight instinct of response. It is then, at that moment, you either fight or run. In most cases, you revert to the fight instinct, and you act violently to attack someone intending to protect yourself. You are trying to protect the inner wounded child from being hurt and feeling powerless, humiliated, and misunderstood again.

Now, we have scenario four, which is another approach to the addiction part. It is when you look at the autonomic nervous system, parts of the body that regulate your instinctive responses that are programmed and overly stimulated with unprocessed nervous energy. This nervous energy is released in acts of violence, bringing calm and relief from built-up nervousness. It can take the form of symptoms such as anxiety, depression, and many other behaviors associated with short-tempered reactions.

Let's have a look at scenario five. So here, we will look at triggers of violence that normally start with humiliation, feeling powerless, loss of control, and deep-seated feelings of injustice. When you had a traumatic childhood, your life experiences formed and shaped negative thoughts in your mind. These negative thoughts can become so dominant that you find yourself in a daily inner violent battle against these negative thoughts. Your self-esteem has been deeply wounded, and a part of you is always subconsciously fighting to protect yourself from these vulnerable emotional memories and wounds.

We have around 90,000 thoughts processed in our minds daily. When we look at how the neural pathways work and the number of memories going through our minds daily, we see at least 60% of those thoughts and memories are parts that are coming forward from the past. So, you see how angry thoughts can also escalate. Therefore, it reinforces feelings of powerlessness, danger, vulnerability, and humiliation. Can you imagine these thoughts constantly looping in your mind? What is it going to do over time?

Now let's also have a look at another scenario that we have. When we consider anger and its addiction, it is also possible for someone to become stuck in a fight-or-flight state. In these circumstances, a person's need for perceived safety may be so huge that they will revert to violence and other forms of conflict to achieve their goals of physical and psychological safety even though the things that made them angry right now are not that big of a deal compared to how they act. The reason they act so immediately and violently is that they are upset. They are short-tempered because they have reached their capacity to suppress their fear of losing control and feeling powerless.

Another scenario here is that violence also comes from feeling trapped and emotionally suffocated by hostile people and circumstances. For example, maybe you express your boundaries, which are never respected, so you physically assert them. It is like you have to dominate your boundaries over people because you feel so powerless, unheard, and invisible to people listening to you.

Unfortunately, it becomes a pattern, and a violent way of asserting boundaries and claiming control. Moreover, asserting dominance also becomes an act of misdirected anger. Then innocent people suffer in the process. Because of that pattern that has now been set in so strongly, you have suppressed your capacity to express your limitations and boundaries and, instead, now physically show them. Here, the physical memory in your cellular muscles is also in sync with these emotions. So, when you feel the emotions, there is already an automatic reaction to physically react, even if you are not consciously aware of it. It is how these patterns become anchored into the emotional body when they are repeated.

In addition, what we fear is what we try to control the most. Normally, when you look at anger and violence, there is a deep underlying fear of being and feeling completely powerless, which also goes hand in hand with the fear of being overpowered and dominated. Now instead of becoming submissive towards people who would make you feel powerless, you go in the opposite direction, and you become violent to assert your dominance and your position to claim control physically. It eventually allows you to avoid circumstances or people that make you feel powerless.

Anger for women

Anger is a natural and immediate response to threats. Many things make people angry. However, for men and women, anger plays a different role. Here, I would like to talk about anger for women in a broad sense. Everyone can get angry, no matter what age or gender they are. However, women may be more likely to get angry because of issues with their mental health, postpartum rage, and mom burnout. The list of causes of women's anger can go on. Society also reacts differently to women's anger.

Anger management for women can look different from what it might look like for men. Let's explore the aspect of how anger serves women and what are the deep-rooted causes behind women's anger.

I had to dive deep into this and look at some blind spots that I had myself. When I sat with this realization that I am someone who struggled with intense anger, I realized how anger defined my personality and my sense of femininity, or at least what my definition of that was. I am not referring to the classical definition of what women should be like because I have my definition. I have a definition that makes me feel the most comfortable. So, I realized how anger has truly served me in my life. It helped me, or at least it gave me the illusion that I am creating and achieving things; people are listening to me and respecting me.

I did not realize the psychological, physical, and spiritual impact on me and my life, especially my relationship with myself. The more I had dived into anger, the more I became "addicted" to it. I used anger to achieve my goals. Anger became my driving force. However, at the same time, I wanted to be happy. I was searching for happiness, but my state of mind was the opposite.

You are canceling out the very thing that you want. Because the more anger you feel, the more anger you invest back into your life. Subconsciously, you also align yourself with people and circumstances that are going to match your anger. Anger just pours over into so many aspects of our life and into our future as well. You are constantly predicting your future and laying it out in the present moment with every action and step you take and every thought and feeling you feel. I did not realize that I had become the hamster in the wheel with anger.

I wanted happiness but needed the anger to get what I needed in order to be happy. Ultimately, I found myself emotionally, physically, and psychologically exhausted. I started suffering from health problems as well. Anger is a very strong emotion, whether it is for men or women.

However, it has a more of a harsher effect on women. I want to dive deeper into women's roles and how anger comes into play. In most cases, women's anger stems from having been in very masculine roles. So it is like being stuck in a state of fight-or-flight, being challenged with a powerful masculine figure in their life, such as maybe a father figure or even a mother figure that was very masculine, perhaps. It suppresses a woman's femininity; it suppresses their softness and gracefulness. It is because, ultimately, when you are treated in a way where you have to fight all the time, you will believe that you have to fight for everything you want. Women's bodies were not designed to hold anger for long periods of time. Men have a higher capacity than women because of ancestral predispositions.

When you are in that fighting state, instead of automatically moving away from it once you have calmed down and realized that the threat is over or that you have accomplished what you wanted to accomplish, you shift your femininity into your masculinity. It is because many women have associated femininity with masculinity in order to survive in a very domineering and competitive environment.

That is because it is within that masculine role that you feel you have power. It is because you feel heard and listened to when you are angry, have to fight for what you want, raise your voice, demand respect, and want to be heard. But everything in life has a threshold. We have a limit and a capacity to cope and deal with anger and the root causes of it.

When this anger becomes a woman's fuel for taking action, then we have a problem. It means a person needs to constantly feel the anger to stay on target with goals. Now that state is incredibly draining. It is draining your immune and digestive systems, and it is stressing your heart and nervous system as well.

You reach the point where you feel like you are running out of emotional resources within yourself to cope with the suppression.

Let's look at inherited anger. Anger problems or patterns may be from your mother or father, which can also come from your generational history. When we face similar emotional stress factors from our relationships and environmental dynamics, it can trigger these old memories, bringing up a surge of strong, inherited emotions, including our emotions, being flooded and merged in with that anger.

If anger is a problem, it also becomes your biggest nightmare because it destroys your relationships with yourself and your feminine essence. It destroys your gentleness and self-compassion. Eventually, looking at it logically, it is all about survival. We sometimes survive when we feel that we can only fight. If we do not fight, we do not survive. Moreover, as we survive and want to progress, it also requires us to change. If our environment does not allow that change, it can fuel the anger even more. Why? Because it triggers feelings of powerlessness.

It is because of associations that we make with anger and observing and seeing how anger has served other people in accomplishing what they wanted. It becomes like a source now being used for us to tap into, to create something. We might feel, deep down, very powerless, hopeless, or a fear of something that we value being taken away.

When you are angry, in this case, your boundaries have been overstepped a very long time ago, and you are now angry and dealing with a situation that is basically now in damage control mode. That is where you find yourself angry because of a boundary being overstepped. Now it also makes it worse, for example, creating potential circumstances where there are consequences that will cause you to have to fight even more.

Now, also, I want to be clear here about the definition of being a woman. I touched on it briefly in the beginning because it has a diverse meaning. It is not about femininity, but how anger influences your truth, characteristics, and biological identity as a woman to become harder and stronger. It could move you away from who and what you want to be. Ultimately, there is no clearly defined definition of what a woman is or should be. The definitive answer will always be what makes you feel like a feminine woman.

What femininity means to you does not just mean makeup, hair, spa, and nails. It goes far beyond that. Femininity is a state of mind.

The definition might not always fit into another woman's perspective. Now we have an important point to consider. What is important is what makes you feel that you are living a life closest to your true, authentic expression as a woman. The message is that it should bring you happiness, freedom and make you feel safe.

So being in a state of anger might give you the illusion that you are free. It is because anger gives you adrenaline, and it gives you cortisol, which then sets off the fight-or-flight. The response then gives you more confidence than you normally would have had. However, look at the price you are paying to maintain the state of this false or perceived confidence that you have to hold on to. You will never find true happiness if you are always angry because these two polarities cancel each other out.

Let's just quickly look at our history now. In our history, men always used to fight, provide and be the leaders. Women used to be the caretakers, the lovers. They used to be the mothers who would heal a broken heart or a wound if someone got injured. That role requires a tremendous amount of empathy and an ability to relate emotionally. It means that women in the past were much more connected to their heart center. The biological makeup developed that way, and it became used to that biological state we now define as femininity.

As time has now changed, the roles are starting to change between men and women. Women are now stepping into very masculine roles where they are not respected, not listened to, and not honored in a way that any normal human being should be. So, they revert to that fight instinct. They revert to becoming masculine because that was men's role in the past, and they still do. It is the role that is respected. So many women feel they must sacrifice who they are to get what they want. However, I love the example of Mother Teresa, a very beautiful, graceful, and well-respected woman. This woman also had boundaries but did not have to be masculine.

When you look at abuse, even in the past, even inherited sexual abuse or physical abuse, the coping mechanism for dealing with abuse is often anger. Feeling a need to fight against life is often the result of being abused. It leaves a person in such a state of powerlessness and feeling unresourceful. Even if you provoke any animal hard and long enough, they will lash out at some point. They will defend themselves. Humans are the same.

My point? A body designed for graceful emotions cannot handle anger for long periods of time. That is why women develop breast cysts and ovary cysts, just to name a few. It's unresolved anger being tapped in to, to move forward in life. I dive deep into psychosomatics of adults in Metaphysical Anatomy Volume 1.

Anger for men

Men and women experience anger completely differently. The answer to that lies within our history. I would love to dive deeper beyond that to look at potential root causes.

Some men are angrier than others, and others are quiet and calm. That depends on what your coping mechanisms are. This coping mechanism I am referring to is more like a symptomatic expression of the underlying anger. In many cases, anger can always come forward in a way that is used as a coping mechanism; it comes forward as a defense mechanism, hence the fight and flight response.

With this anger that comes forward, it can sometimes be used to protect a person who feels vulnerable emotionally. It could come forward as a way of expressing a boundary or getting a message across, especially if that person did not feel heard in the past.

We all have felt angry, and we know that when we feel anger, it is easy to say how we feel. It is also easier to feel more confident because of the adrenaline and cortisol the body is getting ready to defend itself.

Another part here is that many people say anger cannot be inherited. However, it can. If you had an angry father or mother, there could be a part of you that either became like that or you flipped the opposite, wanting to avoid being like them. It depends on which coping mechanism you reverted to as a young child, even if you reverted to being the peacekeeper, and later on, you switched, and then you became the aggressor.

That normally happens when the coping mechanism we have had our whole life starts to fail. It worked at one crucial moment, but then we revert to it because that is what the subconscious mind remembers. However, if it continues to fail over time, it will switch.

As with everything else in life, we also have a threshold. So, if the coping mechanism does not work, you will hit your threshold, shift gears, and switch the other way. So instead of running away, which is more predictable and seen as being the peacekeeper, you will run and fight instead. This was the case for me, and this switch can flip regardless of your gender.

So, when we look at anger, most men feel angry when someone obstructs them. It can be physical, emotional, or psychological. It is because when a man has an intention and when they want to do something, there are hormones released motivating them to take action.

It also stems from our ancestry, where men had to go out, hunt, do something, or build houses. They had a lot of heavy duty and physical work when they put their mind to something. Their body braces themselves with an energetic resource to give that man the energy he needs to act out on his task. It is like a "push" to do something.

That is also why when we get excited about a project, we want to do something, and we work, work, and become workaholics. It is like you cannot switch that switch off. Cortisol is released when we want to do something, however for our ancestors, they had hard laboring tasks. Our tasks have become less strenuous. So, the body is still producing a little too much cortisol when a desire for action is intended by a person. The energy needed for the activity does not match the amount of cortisol released. In this case, there might be too much unused energy. So, what happens? That nervous energy needs to go somewhere.

That is because physical activity is almost needed, especially if the work we are doing is sitting down and working right in front of a computer or behind a desk. It is not physical work where you can go out and walk or run it out.

When you are being creative, it is a very good idea to go for a power walk or a quick 10 to 15 minutes sprint or run to give that predisposition and its effect the body the physical relief it needs and your body can calm down from the cortisol rush.

If you do not do that, energy is carried over into the next day. Now you might not use your energy by sitting in front of a desk again or doing something without real physical interaction. The best way to deal with this is to think of your project and do physical activity. Then go cycling, swimming, running, or surfing. Whatever you want to do and think of it because then it triggers the body, allowing the body to release the overproduction of cortisol.

That energy needs to go somewhere when that emotion builds. It builds, and you feel angry, frustrated, and agitated because your emotions become heightened. It is almost like a pressure pot. It builds, builds, and it builds until it cannot build anymore, and then it pops. The slightest thing can then aggravate you. You might feel oversensitive because all this heightened energy can be very reactive.

Another aspect that I wanted to add here is that many men also respond to anger by immediately wanting to satisfy that emotion. It is almost like wanting to get rid of whatever you perceive as being in the way. It triggers a feeling of fear and being trapped because entrapment is also a biological response for us in the body.

We hate being trapped. However, most of the time, this entrapment is psychological. So, what happens is that the biological body reacts to psychological entrapment because we emotionally feel how we think and vice versa. It can trigger the feeling when we feel mentally and psychologically trapped. It will trigger the fight instinct because now we have to get rid of this entrapment or this perceived entrapment.

The worst case normally is when you cannot see or understand what triggers this feeling of entrapment from your environment. It can create a tremendously great sense of conflict within. That conflict can also start to sit between what you think and what you feel, which creates the split. That normally happens when you cannot identify what makes you feel trapped in your environment. It can be a deep subconscious memory triggered without you consciously realizing what memories your body is reacting to.

It could be that someone did or said something, and a certain type of work and circumstances around you make you feel like that. It could be a relationship or someone's behavior; it could be anything.

It is important to explore why we feel the way we do. It is because we do not feel emotions just to feel them. There is something that is being triggered. The frustrating part is that sometimes the trigger can be a very deep subconscious memory, and they can often be the hardest to establish.

Looking at anger, I would also love to bring together the aspect of men and women and how anger is so different for them.

When we look at men and women, we have the amygdala in the brain that normally gets triggered when we feel threatened, heightened emotions, and distressed.

The amygdala is something like the panic button. It is a very reactive and impulsive part of the brain. The downside is that it has the maturity of a four-year-old. That is why it is so impulsive, because the frontal cortex rationalizes the amygdala when it sets off.

Women's signals and responses to these areas differ from men's because male ancestors' brains have evolved differently. When we look at our ancestral history. They looked for safety in groups and to reduce stress by connecting with others. When men feel angry, they want to detach, and women when they feel angry want to connect by talking about the problem.

That is why women tend to aggravate and make things worse unintentionally, not because they are trying to provoke men, but because they are trying to connect back to the disconnected connection. Thus, anger is the worst response for a woman to deal with because it creates a feeling of distress and disconnection.

Women will try to solve things. They might get angry or fight back because now they are also afraid, but they are fighting back for the connection. They go about it in the wrong way, and it creates more problems. However, the underlying cause is actually to reconnect. The anger and the response from the woman, if it is from an aggressive perspective, is because of fear. On top of that, women's hormones are also dominated by estrogen. So, women have much less testosterone and more estrogen flowing through their brains.

The evolution of the female brain, when you look at this together with the woman's biological makeup makes it much easier for a woman to look for a solution to the conflict, meaning referring to the emotion of anger even if she may have to compromise and make some personal sacrifices to find a solution to the problem. So, our female ancestors might have also competed, sometimes for partners and sometimes for food. However, the primary goals were to find and achieve social support and protection for children to have a roof over their heads.

Now, men are a little different. It is to compete so that they can reproduce and pass on their genes. Our male ancestors were also hunters and gatherers. That is also why aggression back in the day was needed because now they would establish these rules in their hierarchy, competition, and dominance.

When I say rules, it is like an unspoken behavior you will step into if you want to compete, dominate, and hunt. It is like everyone would go into the same state of mind. Also, the testosterone that dominates the male brain now encourages social withdrawal. So, it is the opposite of that of women. Women want to connect, and men want to withdraw.

Men also desire to be left alone, so they sit there and go quiet when angry. It is absolute silence because they do not want to provoke anything from their environment. So, when we look at this now, from a biological perspective, a man is quite uninterested in conversations. They do not want to talk when angry because testosterone decreases a man's desire to socialize.

Testosterone also influences a man to have a tendency to dominate and control to feel safe. So, men tend to be much more programmed and "wired" to feel drawn to roles of authority and independence.

In general, when you look at a man's biological makeup, they want to be respected. When they have respect, they have control, which is what their biological programming is wiring them to strive for in order to survive. This is deep ancestral programming.

Even when you look at the animal kingdom, there are always males competing for that one leadership role. Also, the male amygdala has an incredibly high concentration of sex hormone receptors, including testosterone. These heightened responses might have reflected in the past as to why men are much more prone than women to display anger and feel frustrated and aggressive.

This heightened response might also account for why men are much more prone than women to display anger and feel frustrated and aggressive.

This may be due to the fact that men have more testosterone than women, which is thought to increase aggression and reactivity. Furthermore, studies suggest that the female amygdala responds differently when presented with a situation in which one needs to assess risk or trust others. This difference in response could help explain why women are less likely to display aggressive behavior and why they are better at assessing risk and making decisions based on trustworthiness.

Overall, it seems that the male amygdala is particularly sensitive to certain hormones like testosterone, meaning men may be more prone to displaying anger quickly and feeling frustrated or aggressive in certain situations. However, this does not mean that men cannot control their emotions any better than women can; rather, it could indicate how socialization factors such as upbringing or environment might play a role in how one's amygdala responds to certain stressors and stimuli.

Chapter 10

Healing Your Relationships (Introduction)

Relationships are one of life's greatest gifts and are crucial to happiness and living a full life. They give us a great deal of laughter and, thus, joy. Having someone to assist us during these difficulties can make all the difference. When others cannot be there for you and provide support, your family and friends can. It is crucial to find a strong support system if we still need to get one.

Relationships are a worthwhile investment. Though we all need time alone, we also need relationships and other support to live a healthy and fulfilled life. Having time alone is essential but being alone may be a challenging experience. Relationships reduce feelings of loneliness and isolation that can come from being alone. Good relationships can strengthen various aspects of our life. The better we understand how relationships function, the more we may benefit from them.

Sometimes, we frequently take for granted how personal relationships impact us and how they can alter our lives for the better or, sadly, often for the worst. Everyone knows how meaningful, healthy relationships are for our lives, but only some know how to resolve conflicts in relationships. Not everyone knows how to heal our relationships from past traumas. So, as much as we talk about how important it is to have good, healthy relationships, we also need to be more aware of how problems can start in our relationships.

We need to learn how to solve problems without getting into fights or arguments that make things worse. We all need to figure out ways to heal our relationships. Specifically, we need to look at how we can improve our relationships and recover from any stressful and painful love experiences. Relationships are essential, so finding healthy relationships, improving an ongoing relationship, and healing from a traumatic relationship are essential.

Relationships are what make the world go round. It may be a relationship with your friend, mom, dad, or romantic partner. It can even be your relationship with yourself. Relationship dynamics are everywhere. It also may be a professional relationship at your workplace that is not necessarily a close friendship; it is just a dynamic. So, it does not matter what way you look at this. It is a part of every single aspect of your life. However, we are specifically going to focus on your relationship with your father, your mother, and your romantic partners and preventing relationships that went wrong in the past. I want you to understand how these relationship patterns can help you pinpoint any past wounds or pain points that continue to reemerge.

There may be things in your life or within you that you cannot let go of. There are aspects or habits that you sometimes bring from previous relationships. Sometimes you have habits and patterns that you bring over from how you were raised. You get that into your romantic relationships. Sometimes you may have unresolved stress, perhaps with your parents. Even if your parents were not active in your life, there might still be unresolved stress with them. Our primary focus will be on how these dynamics influenced you and how these patterns are now showing up in your life.

As you mature and progress through different relationships, you might have several experiences that may reemerge as pain points. We are going to look at these pain points. We will also identify where things you sometimes do not realize are bothering you. It is essential to understand why certain things even repeat themselves. We will examine how your relationship with your parents can start to show up in your relationship dynamics. These dynamics can also show up in your relationships with people. Here, however, we will specifically look at the influence of your past relationships on your current romantic relationships.

Your current romantic relationship may not be working well. Perhaps you have a partner that you just broke up with. If that is the case, I would highly recommend my book, "Embrace The Heartbreak," which would be ideal for you.

Letting go is essential since most of our pain and stress are caused by the past. We subconsciously bring a lot of our past stress into our current relationships. Sometimes we carry that baggage with us. Of course, it is not intentional, but old pain points and wounds occasionally bite us up the ass, and that pain boils over into existing relationships. It unfortunately adds fuel to the fire and causes additional problems. In this case, you might find yourself repeating cycles and patterns of the past.

One of the most common reasons for pain and problems in your relationships is conflict with others. You may have conflicts when you and your partner have different opinions. It is normal to have different ideas. However, conflicts arise when your partner forcefully imposes their opinion on you; maybe you set your opinion on them. Perhaps you do not respect and accept your partner's perspective; you want them to get your idea. This behavior is the root cause of conflicts in relationships. For example, you may have conflicts in your interests when you want to do something, but your partner tries to stop you or forces you to do something else. Sometimes you also have specific goals in your life. You might feel a little challenged when someone, maybe your parents, interferes with certain things that you want to do.

That is why certain things play out the way they did because eventually, you end up being with people because of certain things mirroring for you. Maybe your values or boundaries are reflected for you. Perhaps it is your relationship with intimacy, or maybe it is your relationship with love itself. Most of the time, when you look at how these patterns and cycles are playing out, you find the reason why you feel the way you do. These patterns help you understand why your self-esteem and confidence are not as strong. You discover why all levels of intimacy are not feeling as they should. It also may be your fear of connection and commitment that is upsetting you. Whatever the aspects are, there is always a reason for everything. These patterns continue to show up in your life because there may be prior unresolved patterns, stressful cycles, and wounds from your childhood. It can be the patterns where you observed how your parents behaved with each other and also showed up in one way or another.

I have witnessed a lot of conflicts between people. I have seen people having strict arguments and challenges and making childish decisions. I have even seen people making decisions like "I will never get married or be in a relationship" just because they witnessed a conflicting relationship between their parents. So, in this way, our parents and the way they show up towards each other is also laying a foundation for us regarding what we might think about relationships. It is what relationships are about and how they make you feel. After all your stressful circumstances, you try to make things work for you. You try your best not to suffer from a conflicting relationship like your parents did. You do your best not to experience any stressful and unresolved issues again.

However, the memories in your subconscious mind eventually end up in the same cycle. You create conflicts in your current relationships because you see things from a past perspective. You leave no room for new and positive views to make things better. You obviously do not do this intentionally and consciously. However, it is crucial to understand how your experiences subconsciously affect your current life.

You need to see the old patterns and the pain points that influence your current relationships and circumstances. You only suffer if you do not let go of your past pain points. It may be your fear showing up from the stressful events of your past that continue to influence your current thoughts and actions. Thus, you try to do the opposite, so you do not experience the pain that your parents experienced.

This type of behavior is an avoidance behavior. Avoiding problems is never a solution. By avoiding problems, you will only store unresolved tension within you that will continue to show up repeatedly.

If you avoid problems and stick to your old perspectives and pain points, it will not result in the best outcome. All you will have is negativity, fear, and conflicts. It is because you are losing by not healing and not letting go of that unresolved stress that you experienced in your parent's case. That unresolved stress is now playing out in your life in different ways that sabotage your ability to find a good, healthy, perfect love partner. You cannot find a partner who can be fully in alignment with you, with whom you would like to move on in your life, and with whom you would like to work together towards your shared goals.

You cannot see your aspirations with such unresolved problems, pains, and past conflicts. You only know that you do not want to experience what you observed between your mother and father, so you do not want a partner. I also noticed many people who had a relatively healthy relationship with their parents, and their parents also had a relatively healthy relationship with each other. People who have good relationships with their parents have a certain standard of the kind of partner they want to have. So, they have a better and healthier reference point for what a partnership should look and feel like.

On the other hand, the people who come from a home with domestic violence, verbal abuse, and emotional neglect are trapped in negativity unless they improve their foundation and definition of what a relationship is.

So, it is all about having an awareness of what you can have and what you are worthy of. Every single person is worthy of having the love they want; everyone deserves to feel supported and protected; everyone deserves to be treated in a kind and respectful manner. However, it happens significantly less because everyone has their values and opinions. Everyone has their own goals and aspirations for life. So, we are all trying to make it. We are ultimately trying to do our best. Now, when we look at these patterns, it is where you are feeling stuck.

I have noticed while working with people that two things play a fundamentally important role. Number one, what was your emotional state when you met your partner? What were you looking for if you had to go back, think, and look into the past? Maybe you were looking for someone to fulfill your unmet needs? Perhaps you were looking for the emotional support you once had from your ex-partner or a parent. When we meet someone, there is something within us, conscious or subconscious, that we are looking for and trying to obtain in our life.

We are looking for something we do not have any more that is causing a gap in our life. So, we look outside of ourselves to fill that gap. However, a pain point or trauma from our past may compel us to stop wanting to fill that particular gap. So, we push it away; we avoid it. We become entangled with a push and pull dance between what we want and fear.

Comparatively, if we do not have such a good thing absent, that was present in our past, we can have an experience with it; we can feel its pleasure when we meet a new person. For example, you did not have emotional support in your past relationships, but with this new person, you can see and feel how good emotional support is. However, if you are looking for something that once made you feel good, you can build a healthy reference point in the relationship. What should we do in such circumstances? Creating a healthy reference point and having an experience for the first time is a good decision. There is nothing wrong with it.

If there is a need not being met within us, then it is totally fine to look outside of ourselves where someone else can complete that for us. It is normal to look for someone else who can give us the happiness, support, financial security, or love we are looking for. The catch is not become fully reliant on that person for that specific need to be met.

When you look at your highest value in life, it is also important to understand why this is essential to you. Usually, your highest value is the kind of partner that you are looking for so that they can fulfill your needs. So, also, why is that need essential? Have you ever asked yourself what your highest value in life is? For example, for me in the past, my highest value was love.

It was well long before I started my healing journey. I always said love. All I ever wanted was to have the perfect partner to come in, love me, be with me, and stay with me. I never wanted someone who was not kind, who would abandon or throw me away the way my father did. That was my sole highest value in life. Even financial security was not crucial for me; it was healthy love from a good partner. It makes perfect sense when I look back at why that value was significant. Love was my highest value because of my destructive and stressful relationship with my father.

My dad was an alcoholic. He was a self-medicated drug addict and was abusive. I was also the only child, so all the abuse and toxicity just came toward me. So, my association with love, support, protection, and security from a man was very unhealthy, and my pattern continued where I attracted people that were toxic to me. I was conscious of my relationship with my father and knew what real love should feel like. I knew what I wanted it to be, but I could not create it myself. I could not attract it because I was not attracted to the type of people that would give me that same love.

So, I learned my highest value of love was the fundamental thing that kept me locked into this negative cycle of not creating the love I wanted. I was locked into the negative cycle because my association with the value of love was abuse, neglect, and abandonment by a man.

Now, when I think of love, I see it is coming from a repaired place that has healed. My subconscious mind does not dig back into all these subconscious negative memories because the charge is not there anymore. It is now just a memory. There is no biochemical response within the body because the trauma is released and it feels safe again. The body has discharged the memory. So, now the visceral system and the nervous system have been reset. Now my mind only looks for the highest value of love. Moreover, I have noticed now when I look at people, their patterns, and the kind of love they want from a partner or whatever the dynamic or need is, I use love because that used to be mine.

What you need from a partner and your most significant need differ slightly from your values. It comes into two distinct layers. Now the need is what you want immediately. It is not necessarily the long-term vision of how you want to set up your life. It is more about the immediate satisfaction of an immediate need. My immediate need for partners was honesty because it could ensure they would always be truthful to me. Now when I observe this pattern, I realize whenever I had a partner, I always expected they would satisfy this need. The moment I realized that I had to acknowledge the difference between needing honesty from my father and needing honesty for my partner was a game changer.

I stopped projecting the subconscious expectations onto a partner that I expected from my dad. I started to see my partner in a completely different light. I realized they were just a partners and not that my father who could not show up honestly in my life. It was an important realization for me. However, I also understand that a relationship can have other symptomatic problems.

What I just explained to you is the essence of these symptomatic problems. So, there are things that can go wrong in relationships. It can be, for example, an addiction problem. Maybe your partner is a drug addict, or perhaps you have an addiction, but that has not ruined the relationship. Then again, it also raises the question if your mother and father were addicted to something. Did they have addictive cycles they might have been struggling with, or did they bring those addictive patterns into their relationship dynamics?

So, there could also be an aspect playing out here. However, at the end of the day, when you examine addictions, you realize that it is a form of behavior that allows you access to something you cannot feel without it. Therefore, addiction and relationships may serve as substitutes for providing these missing components and emotional resources. I have seen addictions are quite a big problem in many relationships.

Another symptomatic problem in the relationship can be perfectionism. In the relationship case, perfectionism emerges from moments when your parents or your partner's parents emphasize the need to do things in a perfect, ethical, and systematic manner, like military style.

You think if things are not organized, then they are not good enough. You or your partner may also have been persuaded that you are never good enough. So, you both always strive for perfection, which has become your lifestyle. Now you might project onto your partner to show up in a certain way. Or maybe your partner is projecting that expectation onto you. That may be entirely out of your comfort zone, so conflicts may arise between you and your partner. It creates tension because you lack acceptance of who you are and how you would like to do things.

Moreover, a few of the most critical problems in relationships are arguments, abuse, and neglect. Here, I will use my life example once again so I can make this concept clear. When I look back at my relationship dynamic with my father, I see a lot of abuse. So, my association with my most significant value of love was also associated with abuse that became part of my relationship cycles. My relationship cycles incorporated abuse, neglect, abandonment, and rejection because I always felt drawn to people who were abusive, exactly like my father.

I have noticed another symptomatic problem in relationships. This problem is the people who behave and act in unpredictable ways when they love others out of fear. When I say we love people out of fear, I mean we love them, so they do not leave and abuse us. We love them, so we do not lose their support. We love them, so we may not lose financial security from them. Ultimately, we love with the fear of loss. A relationship can start to feel constantly unpredictable because it is based on fear of failure.

Conditional love is another big symptomatic problem in relationships. It is what I would also call manipulative love and manipulative affection. Let me explain. For example, your partner says, "if you lose more weight, I will love and appreciate you more." Maybe you tell your partner, "If you pay my shopping bills, I will love you more." So, in both cases, you and your partner are imposing conditions on each other. It is highly problematic. It is not love, since love is a beautiful emotion that knows no needs or imposed guidelines. You are just manipulating each other with the help of certain conditions. You might not necessarily express your limits in so many words, but they can come forward in relationships through certain habits, actions, and behaviors.

Then the most critical problem we have in some relationships is the lack of boundaries. It is a lack of limits because if you try to express boundaries, you might feel that the person is losing interest in you or that you would lose their love. The lack of boundaries, fear, and unpredictability come together in this situation. They correlate profoundly and intensely. So, we do not express our limits because we do not want conflicts. We want to be the peacekeepers in most cases. Eventually, we do not want to lose love and support and do not want to be alone. Additionally, it raises significant questions. How is your relationship with yourself? Do you have a fear of being alone? What are the things within you that you do not want to feel or deal with if you are left alone?

You may have a distraction in a relationship. Sometimes we use relationships to distract us from how we truly feel about ourselves or the voices, stress, and emotional wounds from the past. The association, or the partner, is not even that important. It is just what they represent. They become the silencer of the voices. They become the silencer of the problems. In this case, you may attract people not necessarily in alignment with you because of this poor relationship with yourself.

So, when your partner shows up, they reflect that mirror, silent voices, stress, and wounds of your past. You create a secondary independent problem apart from the issues that you have and that are unresolved within you. You added more to these issues by bringing someone else into the conflicting picture within you. So, you end up in a cycle where you do not win and feel suppressed. You end up being miserable, and the process continues, and it can even roll into depression. If you continuously have wrong partners that challenge your boundaries and do not express your limitations, your relationship and your capabilities worsen shockingly. Over time, you become less and less confident in your abilities and worth. So, you start making more matches with people who will make you feel inadequate and worthless.

Moreover, apart from boundaries, another symptomatic issue in relationships is the lack of intimacy or fear of intimacy. I say symptoms because these are all just ripple effects of much deeper root causes, which we discussed in the beginning. So, now we have a lack of intimacy or fear of intimacy. This issue can have so many reasons. Maybe there is a fear of being vulnerable. Maybe there is a history of sexual abuse. Maybe there is a history of fear of losing control. Maybe there is a fear of losing your sense of identity. So many things can be the root cause of lack of intimacy. If you have a partner who does not respect your boundaries, intimacy will be a tremendously big problem for you.

Now we have poor communication as another symptomatic problem in relationships. Communication is a fundamental part of a relationship because communication is an expression of you. It is an absolute expression and an extension of who you are; what your beliefs and values are; what is essential to you; and how you show up in your life. When this extension is projected and sent out into the universe, attacked, or ridiculed, we consider that extremely offensive attitude. It feels like that attack affects your identity because communication is an extension of you.

It is an extension of you. It is just a verbalized aspect of your sense of self. Communication can also be problematic due to childhood challenges. Your communication was already suppressed from a very early age. So, your reference point for communication is deeply challenged. You might end up now with a partner that is very introverted or maybe an extrovert. They continue to suppress you because you cannot correctly communicate and step into your vocal power to express how you feel. In this situation, you may develop a fear of communication which could magnify a prior existing fear of communication from your childhood.

Another relationship symptom that we have here is a lack of empathy. Lack of empathy is because the other person does not understand your values. They cannot comprehend your life's struggles or experiences, which may have influenced your behavior and emotions. So, it is not necessarily a lack of empathy. It is more like a lack of understanding. Your partner cannot connect to you emotionally. Your partner's inability to connect to you can also be observed. For example, their behavior can cause you to feel neglected and disregarded.

There is a clear boundary between lacking empathy and actively choosing not to have compassion. They genuinely do not care, which probably means you are sitting with a narcissist.

We have one more relationship symptom problem here, which is control. Usually, control comes into a relationship because it may be based on unpredictability and fear symptoms. Usually, when we pay attention, we end up controlling. We try to control a partner because we might fear losing them. However, the behavior to control them can become quite destructive; it can be very harmful to the partner and the relationship. It is because control triggers the feelings of feeling trapped, unheard, bad, and rejected for who you are, which might not necessarily be the case. It is just because someone has a fear of losing their partner.

If they can control their partner to act and behave in a particular way, they may continue the relationship. Moreover, sometimes there is also the narcissistic approach to control because people may want to control someone to act in a certain way due to their advantages. For example, your partner may benefit emotionally if you act and behave in a certain way. In such a condition, it is not something about the relationship. It is not necessarily about you, but it is about the other person.

Relationships have so many symptomatic problems; excessive criticism is one also one of them. It also relates to control because criticism is frequently used to manipulate, influence, and instill fear. Once a person is in this state of vulnerability and fear, people can manipulate and control that person efficiently. They can do so because they are tapping into that person's greatest fears. These fears can be a fear of abandonment, rejection, or being alone. The extent that some people would go to avoid experiencing these emotions is incredible.

When you look at it from a biological perspective, rejection is one of the people's biggest fears. For example, when you look at your ancestors in their communities. If a person is rejected out of a community, their chances of survival decrease by almost 95%. They have to find food, water, shelter, and protection all on their own, which is a challenge. It is actually a biological fear of dying which is triggered. Cognitively, it does not make any sense. However, through instinctive responses, it triggers the fear of dying. As a result, when the body experiences a heightened state of distress, you feel it, but you do not quite know how to interpret it. However, because you think of the discomfort and pain, you attempt to take action to counterbalance the stress and discomfort instantly. So, you take action to ensure that you do not feel that stress again, which means you surrender to the person's threat, criticism, or manipulation. That is how you can become stuck in a cycle of abuse and criticism as an isolated example.

Relationship conundrums and dealing with them

If you are upset, give your partner time and space to understand things. Please do not fight with them. I love the concept of the "white flag" and the red flag. A "white flag" means you will not fight with your partner over any issue, and you want to let go of the subject.

If you are in an escalating argument, that is not constructive anymore, you are just putting each other down. You are just saying things for the sake of hurting each other, then it's obvious that you cannot find a solution with the same mindset that created it. So immediately, stop. Just say "red flag". Tell them you need help to think right now to come up with a constructive solution. Respectfully, ask your partner to halt the argument, give each other a "red flag" moment, and return to it later. Say, "Can we please talk about it later?

If your partner does not give you that space, you are dealing with a tremendous problem. It could be indicative that you have an emotionally immature partner. You will always find misalignments in all aspects of this type of relationship unless you like being a parent instead of a partner. Are you going to wait for them to grow, become mature, and meet you halfway? Do you want a partner? Or do you want to project? Some people are content to have a project.

Moreover, express remorse towards each other, especially if the person is upset or angry. Maybe you argued, so you need to apologize. Expressing remorse to a partner is an incredible strength. Another positive tip is to negotiate with your partner. You may peacefully discuss things, even if something makes you sad. You can make your partner feel you are listening to them and trying to understand what they are saying. Please do not say that you do not understand them, this only fuels unnecessary inadequacy for your partner. A more graceful response could be, "I am trying to understand the situation." Do you see the difference? Make it about the situation / argument rather than the partner.

Another brilliant response is, "I am listening to you, and I am hearing you." It is the best response in such situations. Then you and your partner can continue to work on rephrasing the challenge until you understand what they need.

Remember, it takes teamwork to make a dream work. Be a team when there is conflict, support each other and find a solution. It is not always one person's duty to fix things. Fix things and find answers together. Without your support of each other, your relationship will not survive. It is just not going to work. I firmly believe in this approach and have always had it in my relationships.

If there was an argument, I always came back with a solution. I always stated a problem with a potential solution. You are the complainer if you declare a problem without a workable solution. Ask your partner to take a break and come back with potential solutions.

Another great tip for improving your relationship is to schedule your regular activities together. It is essential to do things together where you may be, like team building. You could go to do some shopping together. You can go for morning or evening walks.

Another critical strategy to improve your relationship is to talk every night, even if it is just for five or ten minutes. You may be very busy but take time for yourselves where there are no phones and TV. There is nothing but you just talking with each other maybe about your health or your day at work. You may talk about your goals for the upcoming week. You may also discuss something funny that happened during the day. Make your partner feel you are consciously listening to them. It is a beautiful way to reconnect with to your partner.

There is so much more that I can say about it. However, the main point I want you to focus on is looking at your issues and peacefully resolving them. Peace is essential because fighting is never a solution. Take a break, take your time, be in your space and get back with potential solutions.

Let's establish what your relationship foundation is. The clearer you feel regarding this, the more graceful your relationships can be. When we have clarity in relationship to what we want, we can align ourselves with it and recognize when it comes our way.

I am going to ask you a few questions to help you gain that clarity.

Step 1: What is your highest value in relationships?

_____

Step 2: Does your partner respect this value?

_____

Step 3: Who challenged this important value in the past?

_____

Step 4: Do you feel you need this value to be respected by the person from the past who disrespected it or your partner?

_____

Step 5: What is the greatest need from your partner?

_____

Step 6: Is this need an unresolved pain point from your childhood? If so, which person did you need this need from the most?

_____

Step 7: Do you feel you subconsciously needed your partner to fulfill this need?

_____

Step 8: What were you looking for in a partner?

_____

Step 9: What did you get after you met your partner?

_____

Step 10: Is the above answer in Step 9 a pattern you often find yourself in with relationships?

_____

Step11: If your answer at step 10 was yes, then do you feel it's possible that you have an association with Step 8 being met with Step 9? This could be an important association to resolve in order to break your negative relationship patterns.

_____

Relationship affirmations

I call my power back from partners who failed to recognize my self-worth in the past.

I call my power back from partners who disrespected me in the past.

I call my power back from partners who failed to acknowledge and see me the way I wanted.

I call my power back from partners who made me feel trapped in the past.

I call my power back from partners who made me feel suppressed in the past.

I reclaim my identity and sense of self within relationships.

I reclaim my happiness within relationships.

I reclaim my balance within relationships.

I reclaim my inner peace in relationships.

I reclaim my boundaries within relationships.

I reclaim my self-respect in relationships.

Chapter 11

Change how old trauma and anger effects your relationships

At some point in life, we all suffer from tremendous stressful events that cause trauma. Trauma may destroy our sense of security and leave us feeling powerless. It can also leave us with distressing feelings, memories, and persistent anxiety. Additionally, it may make us feel detached, apathetic, and hard to trust other people. We may think that trauma can affect our life for as long as it stays, and its effects from our life disappear as soon as the stressful events go away.

For example, physical trauma in the form of a physical injury heals as soon as the wound heals. However, trauma is much more than that. It can have long-lasting effects on several important aspects of our future life as well. Trauma becomes stored in our body and does not go away even after happening. So, it influences us in several ways that we may be unaware of. For example, we may have seen a horrible car accident a few years ago, so we are still scared to drive a car.

Similarly, there may be several old traumatic events that may still be affecting us in many essential aspects of our life. An old trauma maybe even affects our relationship with other people. It sounds strange, but it is true. An old trauma can negatively affect our relationships. However, we have the power to change the way it affects our relationships.

I particularly want you to focus on the effects of old trauma on our relationships. Therefore, we need to see how old trauma affects our relationships and how to start to swing that around. We can begin by getting awareness about this problem. As we all know, knowledge is power, so awareness can effectively help us change how old trauma affects our relationships. We often unconsciously think that communication is what makes the world go round.

However, in actuality, it is through the relationships that the world continues to revolve. Communication and many other things keep moving the world forward, but relationships play a tremendous role.

Relationships can take a lot of energy out of us, especially unhealthy ones. In any relationship, there may be a lot of strain, stress, and unresolved things. Whatever the pain points are for us, if they are causing stress, it means our body is also under stress. For example, we can have psychological stress because of our relationships that also cause physical stress in the body. So our health is also going to suffer. We consciously need to understand how trauma affects our relationships with others and ourselves. We also need to know how trauma can affect many other essential aspects of our life, including our emotional, mental, and physical health.

Before looking into the effects of trauma, let us first see what trauma is. Trauma leaves us feeling out of control, unsafe, and powerless. It instills a tremendous and resourceful feeling that we cannot overcome a bad situation. It also makes us feel that we cannot heal from stress.

Even a little traumatic event can leave a long-lasting effect on us that negatively affects our quality of life. It means trauma alters our quality of life for an extended time, even after it has occurred. It is almost like we cannot return entirely to who and what we were and how we were living our life. Trauma alters our thought patterns and our emotional state as well. So, when we look at the effects of trauma, we can see that trauma affects our relationships and emotional, mental, and physical health.

Now let us see what a relationship is. A relationship is a beautiful dynamic between two people with a mutual understanding of ease and grace. The mutual sense of ease and grace is so important in relationships because we will have conflicts and negativity without it. So, keep in mind that there is always a beautiful and peaceful relationship where there is mutual understanding, mutual respect, and clear and respectful communication. If both parties feel safe, they will feel fulfilled in the relationship.

So, it also depends on what kind of relationship we have with others, whether it is a friendship or a romantic relationship. It is also important for us to see where our pain points are in a relationship, where those pain points fit in for us, and how they can ultimately benefit us.

We also need to understand the concept of discord in a relationship. Discord can happen due to something that does not go as planned, when someone disappoints us, or there is a traumatic event, etc. When there is discord in relationships, there are unresolved wounds. Discord disrupts the connection of a relationship.

How would you define a connection? Well, a connection is something that makes us feel connected, delighted, uplifted, loved, and valued in a relationship. Without a connection in a relationship, we may feel lonely, isolated, ignored, or invisible. Due to a connection in a relationship, we feel heard, seen, loved, and valued, like an integral part of a family, group of friends, or working environment.

So, the connection is all about feeling included and valued. Looking back at our ancestors and their lifestyles, we can see the connection was everything to them. A strong connection was everything for our ancestors because it kept them interconnected. A connection is, in fact, necessary because if we are abandoned or kicked out of a community, we can be triggered by the fear of death.

Surprisingly, the fear of death is something we have, even today. It is why we fear rejection. Many people choose to stay in toxic relationships because they fear rejection and being abandoned and kicked out. However, the problem is not the fear of rejection; instead, the subconscious, old ancestral trauma and memory trigger us. Moreover, this old ancestral trauma and memory is the fear of dying as a result of abandonment. It is why a lot of people decide to stay in highly toxic situations. People think they cannot break a relationship at any cost. In actuality, their subconscious mind frequently tells them they will die if they break a relationship. It is the ancestral memory speaking in their subconscious mind. Conversely, people who choose to leave a toxic relationship think they can leave because they can learn how to survive after breaking up from a relationship. They learn different coping mechanisms that help them deal with such a difficult situation.

In addition, when we have a connection, we know there are emotional, physical, psychological, and intellectual connections. The term connection is quite broad, so it is also important to look at our pain point in terms of connection. It would be great to consciously think about it and write it down on a notepad.

Start by thinking, what is your definition of relationships? What relationship dynamics would you like to look deeper into right now to start to resolve your life quickly?

My relationship definition:

_____

The next point you should consider and write about your pain point in terms of the connection you have in your relationship that you would like to address. Is your relationship too much of an emotional dramatic connection, or does it lack an emotional connection? Is your relationship an intellectual connection, a romantic connection with no intellectual connection, or a friendship connection? The list of connections is long, and it can be absolutely anything. The types of connections are not limited to what I just said.

My relationship dynamics are:

_____

My next question to you is: "Which emotional connections were absent from your childhood?"

Answer: _____

How did you respond to that?

_____

Is that the same disconnection being repeated in your relationships?

Yes, or no? _____

What is the most significant pain point in your relationships?

Answer: _____

How did you respond to that?

Answer: _____

Are you responding the same way you did in your adolescent years?

Answer: _____

It is fine if the type of connection and pain points are different; note it down.

Now, think of the kind of people that you have been attracting in your life. Often, we attract people based on our most significant wounds. It is because when we go through trauma and painful moments, we do not entirely resolve the pain point, and our subconscious mind remembers this painful moment.

Answer: _____

I invite you now to think and write about the stress or pain points you feel in your relationship.

Answer: _____

What is the positive flip side of these points?

Answer: _____

When you finish writing your answers, write the opposite scenario of these answers. My answer:

_____

Relating to the above answers you just wrote, what is stopping you from giving this to yourself?

Answer: _____

What steps can you take to start today to give this to yourself, so you no longer have to seek this from a partner who is outside of you?

Answer: _____

I trust you can see the power in these messages.

Chapter 12

Relationship with Father

If we have healthy relationships, then our life is significantly more pleasant. We have a diversity of relationships in the form of friends, parents, siblings, teachers, or coworkers. However, our relationship with our parents is the most important, and it significantly impacts many aspects of our lives. It is because we frequently relate several aspects of our life with our parents. For example, we relate our partners in our relationships to our parents.

If we want to build a new way of relating to our partners in our relationships, it is important that we lay solid foundations for our house: our being, which comprises our body, mind, emotions, and spirit. Occasionally, this requires laying whole new foundations. First, we realize that our bonds with men and women as adults are based on our first interactions, which are our parents. We need to look at how we got along with our parents to understand how we get along with others and how we get along with ourselves.

Here, I specifically want to focus on our relationships with our fathers. Our relationship with our fathers as children and adults significantly impacts our capacity to maintain fulfilling and committed relationships, find fulfillment in our careers, feel empowered and express ourselves. Our relationships with our fathers are a profound bond. This relationship has a profound and lifelong impact on us as a child and throughout our adulthood. Numerous aspects of our personal lives and well-being are tied to our relationship with our fathers, although we may not realize it.

I met many people from different backgrounds, and the problem that came up most often was relationship problems caused by unresolved "father challenges." A problematic relationship with a father can equally affect the relationships and attitudes of males and females toward their partners.

Often, in homes where the father fits one of the above-mentioned categories, the mother is the front-line parent who is predictable, present, and familiar. In contrast, the father is periodic. Even though the roles of parents are changing in modern society, the father is usually the primary provider for the family and feels responsible for their survival. He leaves for work either before or soon as the children awaken, and he returns when they are going to bed. Occasionally, he travels for work for multiple days or weeks.

Our relationship with our father shapes how we view ourselves and the people we care about. It affects how we interact with others and decide important things about ourselves, our life goals, and our core beliefs. A father is one of the child's first links to the outside world and all the worries and decisions that come with it. The recognition that fathers play such a crucial role is relatively recent.

For many years, the primary focus has been on mothers and how they affect their children's physical, emotional, and spiritual health. Long ago, the parental role of a father was excluded from this equation, as his task was not to nurture but to earn. Fathers may be aloof or affectionate, harsh or fair in judgment, devoted or uncommunicative. However, little thought or consideration was given to how these disparities might affect us as children.

This topic is very close to my heart because it has been my journey. I had a very challenging relationship with my dad from day one, when I started understanding my surroundings as a child until he passed away. It is a sensitive topic, but also one that is tremendously important since the role that our fathers play in our lives is tremendous. Obviously, the role of mothers in our lives is also important; the role of both mothers and fathers as parents is significant.

As we progress through this topic, you will start to understand not just the emotional connection, but also the impact of the biological link to our fathers. You will begin to know how our father's presence or absence in our lives can enormously affect our biological, emotional, and psychological development. You will start to understand how our father's role in our life impacts how we show up in our lives and what type of decisions we make.

The absence of your father in your life has the same impact on you as their presence does. However, some fathers play a positive role in their child's life, while others have traumatic experiences for their children. So, it does not matter if your father lacked compassion, was abusive, or completely absent. Maybe your dad passed away when you were young, or they abandoned and rejected you. Whatever the dynamic you have with your father doesn't matter. What matters is how that dynamic affects you. I want you to see your relationship with your father closer and how it impacts you in various aspects of your life.

So, let's start. What does having a father mean to you? What is your definition of having a father? When I say definition, I mean how a father looks and feels to you. Please focus on the definition based on what you want and need from a father. Since this definition will show you some aspects that are missing from the aspects you already have, let's write your definition of having a father. While writing your definition of father, please forget about the ideas and opinions that society or media portrays about the role of a father. Forget about the books you have read; forget about what your friend's father is like. Just write the definition based on what your needs are right now from a father. Forget what you wanted from your father in the past and focus on what you want right now.

Definition: _____

Now you have your definition. Please reread this definition. Please highlight those parts you do not have with your father and keep this definition note aside.

Now focus on those aspects you have experienced with your father and the needs he was able to fulfill.

Answer: _____

When we look at the biological history of a father figure, we see they are usually the protector, the provider, the alpha male, the leader, and the one who makes decisions. Our biological makeup has a certain level of expectation of what is logically needed from a father; it is not a conscious expectation.

However, in modern societies, fathers are diverse and different from the expected biological makeup. It is because society has changed, and so expectations have changed. Now, we have mothers who sometimes perform as "alpha males", mothers who are the household's primary caretakers and decision-makers, and mothers who support the entire family. You can see it is a complete reverse of traditional roles.

Let's look at the positive role of a father figure from a biological perspective. Let's say a father figure helps build your confidence, character, identity, and self-worth. This firm, positive, and healthy relationship with a father figure has a tremendously significant impact on your self-worth and your overall well-being. Your strong and healthy relationship with your mom also affects you positively, but the effect of your father's role is more significant than a mother's role.

So, when you look at how your relationship with your father shows up psychosomatically in your body, you might often find a lot of tension in your back and solar plexus area. We typically store stress with our fathers in the sternum. So, when you sometimes feel emotional stress or maybe issues around your self-worth, power, identity, and confidence, you usually feel it in the heart and solar plexus.

Now, when you look at the confidence aspect and how healthy your relationship with your father is, you can observe it has a direct impact on how strong your confidence is. You can observe that your healthy relationship with your father directly affects how healthy your identity is and how strong your belief systems and values are. It directly impacts how much you believe in yourself and how strong, confident, and safe you feel.

So, this is why when you look at your dynamic and connection with your father now, especially from a biological perspective, you think the father plays the role of the alpha male in the house. You think they are leaders and decision-makers. That is just logical reasoning based on our ancestral history and patterns.

When we look at the patterns of our ancestry, I am focusing so much on the biological part because the biological body plays a much more significant role in what you select as partners and how you emotionally feel about these relationship dynamics. Emotions are often suppressed because of biological selection and alignment with a partner based on your biological associations made with a father figure.

Also, the patterns that play out from generation to generation are very much based on your entire past life; your biological body carries the history of your ancestry. You are an expression of your ancestors. Ancestral patterns will inevitably surface in your life. This can be a leading factor as to why you might constantly seek approval and safety from an alpha male. Your body is programmed to search for guidance and support from an alpha male because your father was meant to fulfill these basic needs. It has a direct impact on your self-worth.

Due to these patterns, your biological body indicates that you are worthy of being protected, supported, and guided. It means you are worthy of being loved and included because you might have a trauma associated with being rejected by your father.

You also have an inherited trauma because when you look at society, especially your history and ancestors when they lived in communities, men were normally in charge. They were the leaders, decision-makers, and alphas, and the women were their followers. Now the programming of that history is still fresh in the biological body because it takes the biological body many generations to shift and change.

It is evolution, and it takes time to adapt to new ways of life. Our frontal cortex can adjust within seconds, but the biological body has a tremendous delay in how fast it can respond and how quickly it can be programmed because of our survival responses. Let's understand this concept from the perspective of when you heal.

You work on yourself and influence certain epigenetic and biological expressions, and you successfully calm down or completely switch off specific emotional traumas. That's a good enough job. However, if those expressions stay switched off for at least a hundred to 200 years, does that reflect only then? Does that healing holds permanently and gets programmed into the DNA? Yes, it does. That is how long evolution can take to make a permanent change in your DNA lineage.

It is now precisely my point that society has changed recently. It has changed only in the last 20 to 30 years in relationship to men and women roles. That is why a big part of the biological body is still trying to adapt. It is why your biological body is also trying to find its way around. Your biological body is trying to figure out, "How do you connect with a father figure? How do you connect with the alpha that is the leader? Who is the leader in the house?"

You can also see in society that the traditional and biological father figure has drastically changed from what our ancestors were. It is a considerable change.

In society and on social media, you can see how fathers are now portrayed as different types of fathers. Society is completely accepting this change. Now, cognitively, we can adapt to this change fast. However, the biological body will always feel that something is missing until this pattern is repeated again and again over generations, maybe a hundred to 200 years. Only then can the biological body adapt and feel fully comfortable with this new change because it can sense the connection with the "father," whomever that may be at the end of the day. It requires no cognitive interference. The biological body consents to leadership, protection, and support. The body has a consciousness of its own. When you look at this consciousness, connection, and dynamic that the biological body feels from a father figure, you see you can have not only mental trauma but also trauma stored in the visceral body, through the instinctive responses, through the biological body.

It is why sometimes when we look at the connection with the father or healing the relationship with the father, it can run very deep. It can be quite complex because sometimes we deal with certain aspects connected to the relationship with the father. Still, we miss certain other elements, which might be the biological aspect of the father. This is why the biological part is tremendous. Also, this is why "relationships with fathers" is a tremendously important topic for me.

Now I am sharing a few more essential points with you. When we look at the roles of our fathers, we see some father figures appear very feminine. I have seen a lot of fathers who show up very feminine presence. We can also see the feminine presence of father figures in our ancestry. Some father figures appear feminine, whereas the mother might have more of a masculine approach. Mothers may have more leadership; they may be more controlling or the ones supporting the family. They may be more of the decision-makers; for example, only they will decide how to live and act in the home. So based on these, you observe how the father figure is showing up in your life. Even the absence of a father figure significantly impacts your self-esteem.

Moreover, regardless of whether the dad is feminine or masculine, their presence or absence has a tremendous effect on several aspects of his life. If your father had a very feminine approach in his dynamic with your mother and with you, you might be a lot more masculine, a fighter, a supporter, and a leader.

It is only sometimes the case because your father might have been very masculine, aggressive, or abusive. There was a part of you that had to match that for survival. It is because being the peacekeeper would not have helped you to survive. So, this is just another component as well. However, if you look at that, perhaps being feminine, you might notice yourself as more masculine.

If you find that to be true for you, it is because the biological body is trying to compensate for something it wanted from the father figure, but it could not get that. So, it is trying to compensate for the absence of that need because it is programmed to look for that. It is programmed to set the "antennas", to feel and relate to the dynamic with the father, and to develop based on feedback. If it is not there, the biological body will create the base on prior subconscious memories based on ancestors who had a father connection. It will also seek out a figure in its immediate environment to relate to. The body will try to create that connection for itself.

Observing and seeing how it can show up in your life is also interesting. It is exciting to follow that dynamic with data, regardless of whether your father was present in your life or not.

No father wakes up thinking, "How can I ruin my child's life to the best of my ability?" Most fathers do not do that. The way that your father showed up in your life was the way that his father showed up in his life. So, if we look at whatever was happening between your father and his dynamic with his father, there is a very high chance that your father can now be repeating his father's dynamic with you. It is not the case for everyone, but there are high chances since it is their best and earliest reference point regarding how to show up as a father.

However, the most beautiful thing that is also happening in today's society is that many fathers and new fathers are consciously and actively trying to heal themselves. They are healing their dynamics and relationships with their fathers so that they can avoid repeating the same inevitable mistakes with their children.

Let's now say this was not the case for you. For example, your father did not have the opportunity or the tools to heal his relationship with his father, but at least through conscious action, he tried to behave better. He tried to make better and different decisions, but there were moments when he failed. There were moments when he did not always get it. Your father could not make it up for particular moments, things, or circumstances. Ultimately, you cannot change how your father showed up. That is now done and dusted. That is now in the past, but the good point is what you can change.

What you can change is how this affected you and how this made you feel in your life. You can change how it emotionally and psychologically affected you. It is a fundamentally important point before we move on to the healing part. So, when I look at the relationship dynamics with fathers, I always remember that I learned something significant in my life. That is, there is a difference between surrendering to the way your dad was and the way he is showing up and being in a place of acceptance. I had to learn to accept my father the way he is. He was an alcoholic and a self-medicated drug addict, and I had to accept it. He was a medically diagnosed sociopath. It was a very tough relationship.

So, you can imagine, I had a lot of resentment towards him. There were a lot of pain points and substantial unresolved trauma and stress. A big part of me was always wishing for my father, "why could you not be like this? Why could you not be like that? Why could you not be like my friend's father?" Just this significant part of me always wished for my father to be different.

A part of me subconsciously punished him for not being the way I needed him to be. So, I learned in this dynamic with him that there is a big difference between accepting someone and surrendering to them. It is just my opinion. Surrendering means giving up; you feel completely powerless and hopeless toward that person. You take the path of least resistance, becoming the victim of the circumstances. I have always been fighting hard my whole life not to take the victim's stance for me. I see it as an absolute failure. I dive deep into this in my biography, "Unveiling My Truth".

So, I accepted my father for being the way he was. I accepted that he did not have any emotional resources or conscious access to emotional resources within him to behave in a good way. I accepted the fact that he was always going to be an alcoholic and a drug addict. Though there was also another minor part of me and a little voice in me that said, "Always try to see good in him and always try to see his highest potential." It was hard!

Here is a different take on it. Have you ever spoken to someone who left you deeply inspired and confident? Or you talked to someone who left you deeply frustrated, irritated and degraded even though the person did not do anything, but you just felt like it was not a great conversation. You might have just walked away feeling a little negative. Two things could have happened at that point. Either they felt negative, and that influenced their conversation with you. Or maybe they had a negative thought about you or something you said. Then you have people who felt positive before they spoke to you, and you could feel that positivity, which left you feeling positive after a conversation. Or they saw your best self, and they held positive thoughts about you. Either way, you are intuitive enough to sense whether a conversation is positive or negative, right?

Because of this power we have with our attitude and how it can translate into a conversation, I decided to always hold the highest potential for my father when I spoke to him.

It was hard, as all I could think of was how he failed me. It was a conscious shift in my consciousness I had to make. I knew he could show up in a good way, but he did not have that capacity based on the tools and experiences he had in his life. So, I had to accept that things are just the way they are. I had to accept that he was the way he was and would not change. It does not mean you have to accept the abuse, negligence, emotional absence, abandonment, or rejection. It is not what I am saying. What you are accepting is just your father being the way he is, and it is out of your control.

It is an acceptance of someone with their mistakes and flaws. However, this acceptance means the conscious realization that someone could not rise to the level of your expectations and your definition of being a father that you wrote earlier.

So, just because your father might not have been able to rise to that level is not a reflection of what you are worthy of. I repeat that your father could not rise to the level where you needed him to be; it is not a reflection of what you are worthy of. Your father could not rise to that level because of his blockages and lack of references to what genuine, authentic, and safe love should look and feel like. Perhaps their father was absent from them because of a divorce, death, or emotional disconnection. Maybe there was some physical distance. There can be many reasons. However, whatever you needed, there was a part of you calling your father to step into a specific role that he could not do. If he did, he would have.

Now maybe your father was not necessarily abusive. Perhaps he was just emotionally absent. Well, it is an excellent example once again. If he had the emotional capacity to connect to and be with you emotionally, then he would have emotional resources and conscious access to emotional resources. What prior reference do you have to act or react if it is not there? It is also about what a father might value. In terms of what a father should be, their values can also differ from yours.

He might think that he has done everything right, and you might feel that he has been doing everything wrong. Your father's values are based on his upbringing and on what is important to him. So, it is not necessary that what is important to them should be important to you. You and your father might have different experiences in life. So, your father's values are also shaped by their experiences.

My father's value was about financial survival to the point where I did not exist, and my value was to have a present masculine figure in my life. Now I am just asking for a father figure whose highest value is to survive to be emotionally present with me. There is a substantial incongruent right there already. We could not see eye to eye because the motivators driving us were so different.

Moreover, because he could not meet my needs in a way, I needed him to be was not a reflection of what I was worthy of. It was a reflection of what my father was capable of based on his values, childhood experiences, and life experiences. It was a reflection of another crucial aspect here that I learned from my journey.

Moreover, my experiences with my father and my need to have him emotionally attached to me and show up in a certain way completely ruined my life. It destroyed my ability and capacity to heal. So why am I talking so much about this? Because my dynamic with my father challenged my future relationships with partners. I am sharing this to help those of you see the potential bigger of why you might have certain relationship patterns playing out.

So, my past with my father ultimately held me back from moving forward because my emotional attachment to the need to have a specific experience with him was so tremendous. I could not let this emotional attachment go. The fact that I could not let go of my wounds with my father meant that there were certain aspects and patterns that I kept repeating in my relationships with men and relationships with my career. I kept repeating certain elements and patterns in my relationship with myself. My emotional attachment to him was to be the father I always needed him to be, which ruled my life.

So, I had to withdraw that attachment because my emotional attachment to see him in a certain way was based on someone that could not meet me halfway. All my past partners mirrored this frustration back to me. I kept attracting people who were exactly like my father.

It is a significant realization to have today. It is a powerful conscious realization to make. The day I withdrew my emotional attachment to the need to have my father behave in a certain way was when I felt my emotional freedom. That is when I found my emotional liberation, and I was able to recognize healthier partners in my life.

That is when I started feeling and experiencing joy because my attachment overshadowed everything. To feel this emotional boundary that I was trying to have with my father, I needed to feel all the anger, resentment, remorse, and everything else that was going on. I needed those emotions because that is what fueled my resentment, and the resentment fueled the realization and the conscious boundaries that I was trying to have with my father. I could not have limitations with him without anger. You can see the trap. It became a vicious cycle, and my attachment cycle almost placed the same type of role.

We need to feel this way. We try to get our father to meet us in a certain way, but he cannot; it is a self-fulfilling prophecy. It is because our emotional needs cannot reinforce our self-esteem, so this emotional need slowly disappears before we know it. It is how we perceive our identity as worthy. However, breaking that attachment cycle strengthens your relationship with yourself and your self-esteem boosts.

I would like to ask you a few questions to help you get clarity.

What did you need from your father?

_____

How are you trying to obtain this from your relationships?

_____

What steps can you take to release your partner from fulfilling a role they are not responsible for?

_____

There is tremendous power in these answers. These answers will assist you in building healthy relationships that are not based on old wounds but bringing forward your greatest self.

Chapter 13

Relationship with your mother

This world is full of blessings. The most significant blessing we can have is to have healthy relationships, particularly a strong and positive relationship with our mother. Our mother is the one who gave us life. She cared for us as a child and did everything she could to give us the best life possible.

Most mothers will always be there for their children. Whether it is a bad day, an argument with our partner, or a problem at work, our mother will always listen, console, and guide us.

A mother-child relationship can be complicated, but it is still one of the most valuable bonds between two people. Mothers provide us with gifts and insight into life in various ways. Unfortunately, because of how our mothers may have "poorly" treated us in the past, we frequently ignore some of these gifts and blessings. They may have also treated us with immense love and kindness. However, I want you to understand how our relationships with our parents affect us in our entire life. How do these relationship dynamics play themselves out throughout our live? Undoubtedly, the role our parents play in our life directly impacts several aspects of our lives. It is essential to understand this relationship with our parents a little closer.

Most of us have unique, friendly, and lovely relationships with our parents. Some of us are closer to our fathers, and some are more attached to our mothers. In both cases, our parents equally influence our lives. However, here I want to dive into our relationship with mothers because we always have a different and deep attachment to them compared to our fathers. It is also because we have already spent the first nine months of our life and our complete development with her. When we look at this beautiful divine connection that starts from such an early developmental stage, we see a lovely connection, especially on a biological level.

When you look at when you were in the womb and had not yet developed your cognitive functioning or awareness, you realize your body already had a sense of awareness that your mother is with you. This feeling of the presence of your mother for you right from the day you were born plays a big role throughout your life and built such a fundamental key point in your foundation and your relationship with yourself.

How your mother showed up in your life can affect your relationships and your relationship with yourself. Maybe she was absent. Maybe she was abusive, or she passed away early in your life. We will not focus on these aspects too much because its outcome can be tremendously diverse.

However, we will focus on how it made you feel, how it affected you, and how these patterns and these cycles played out in your life as you matured and grew up. We will immensely focus on how it affected you as you built other relationships in your life. It is because you already know that your relationship with your mother and your father or their absence also pours over into your relationship with other people, especially with romantic partners. Your relationship with your parents can also show up and reflect in your professional and friendship relationships.

When we look at the overall connection with our mothers, I would like you to write your definition of a mother. When you write your definition, please forget about the ideas and perspectives that society or media portrays about what a perfect mother would be like. Forget about what your friend's mom was like. Please focus on and write the definition based on how you wanted your mother to show up and what you needed from her.

Definition: _____

Once you have done that, just set that definition note aside.

Let's come back to the role of the mother. We will first focus on the role of a mother from an ancestral perspective. It is imperative to understand that the role mothers used to play in the past and the way they are showing up now are tremendously different. When we look at the ancestor and how mothers show up, we see they were the caretakers; they supported the family emotionally and always prepared food for the family. They were there to give you compassion and love to nurture you. They were there to guide you in a way that a mother would.

In most cases, mothers were usually the kind witness, the supporter, and the ones who held the family and everyone together. However, not all mothers showed up in that way. Some moms were very masculine. Some moms were showing up as the leader or decision-makers. Moreover, some mothers also showed up aggressively.

Typically, most of the mothers showed up as caretakers and supporters of the family. So, what happens is that the biological makeup is programmed, and it is a mother's fear of showing up in this way. We have the biological body programmed to have food, water, shelter, and also a certain amount of emotional comfort that helps the biological body to develop to its fullest potential. It comes from the dynamic with our mother as well. Now, what happens? Is that a part of our ancestral programming? The ancestral programming is now where the biological body expects mothers to act a certain way because of historical programming. The biological body seeks to have that experience with the mother as you grow, mature, and develop.

When a mother figure cannot step up to that or fulfill that biological need that you are looking for, the body perceives it as a lack and a shortcoming. It can trigger a sensation and feeling of distress because it does not receive the nurturing it is wired for biologically. If the biological body is distressed, it will cognitively translate into tension, stress, or even anxiety. It can even come forward in the form of feeling overly needy. So, when we look at this pattern and how it can all play out, we see the biological body has a way of developing slower than the cognitive mind and frontal cortex. The frontal cortex can grasp changes instantly, but the biological body cannot because the biological body is very much connected to our historical evolution.

From the part "Relationships with Fathers," you might remember I was talking about how the frontal cortex develops and evolves almost instantaneously. Still, the biological body takes a little time to grasp the changes. However, your frontal cortex suddenly shifts because your environment is different. It adapts. However, the biological body has a tough time adapting at such a rapid pace and is still struggling to grow to its total capacity.

When we look at this dynamic and connection with our mothers, we know we had this connection with her before birth. We know our mothers were with us from day one of our development and conception. However, this connection and her presence that we had right from the beginning separated after our birth. It is a healthy separation. The separation is meant to take place, but there is an adjustment phase for the body to feel comfortable with the absence of the mom's connection and presence. To find your individuality during that moment after your birth, you felt safe within your sense of self on your own. That is because you are introduced to your independence.

Now that independence might be a bit stressful. It can also be graceful and smooth. It depends on our mother's role toward us. We all have different transition periods. However, when we look at having that connection with our mother, we start to interpret and perceive our mother as almost a subconscious God-like figure because she gave life to us. She is the most familiar reference point you can have because she was there from the beginning. She also nurtures and looks after you after your birth. So, your connection with your mother is on and off because when she is physically present with you, you recognize that familiarity, but when she is away, you feel that absence.

I have learned from my knowledge that our body holds the psychosomatic stress of different ailments in different areas of the body. So, it is essential to see how accumulated stress can play a role and how the biological body responds by letting you know which emotions have been suppressed. Now, when you look at mother's connection and absence, you interpret it as the absence of God and the absence of something greater outside of you that has power. It is true, significantly, if your trauma with your mother sometimes overlaps with your religious beliefs and perspectives about God. Here, you might feel a lot of abandonment and stress associated with feeling abandoned, not good enough, unworthy, and unseen by God if you feel the same way about your mother.

It highlights the critical question, "How was your relationship with your mom?" This question will already summarize a tremendously significant explanation for you right there in terms of what your relationship is like with God if you are religious.

When you look at your connection with your mother now, for example, the psychosomatic stress of where you store your relationship with your mother, you will generally look at the stomach area. That is where you store your psychosomatic stress and unresolved trauma with your mother. So, how you feel profoundly correlates with how you felt while in your mother's womb. It is because your mother's emotions already had a tremendous overlapping impact on you from the beginning. This is a scientific fact.

I have been teaching for many years now that the placenta in the mother's womb is not a barrier between the mother and the child. So, your mother's emotions have a tremendous overlapping impact on you from the beginning. It has now started to be recognized. Scientists now realize that the protein cells in the lining of the placenta absorb the mother's stress. These protein cells are responsible for your development. It says a lot! Let that sink in.

However, putting that aside, we may now look at the stress we feel in the stomach. Generally, if you have stomach ulcers, you have a lot of tension in your stomach. You might have a lot of gastric acids. Now we are looking at a very stressful relationship with the mother that might not necessarily be abusive. It could be a relationship where the mother was very controlling and a strict parent. It may also be a relationship where the mother was absent, or maybe she was very abusive. Whatever that dynamic was, that stress would sit right in your stomach. Now, when we look at the stomach area, it very closely correlates to the solar plexus and the sternum.

Now the sternum relates to our relationship with our father and how healthy that relationship showed up in these areas. It also shows up emotionally in the form of how confident you feel. Your confidence and self-worth are also directly connected to how healthy your relationship was with your mother. If there was a lot of stress, you can see how that could have translated and is probably translating to your relationship with yourself and other people. You can understand how that stress translates to how confidently and strongly you show up in your life and relationships. It is because if you have a stressful relationship with your mother, you might be having a lot of trouble having a healthy amount of regard, awareness, and mindfulness toward your emotional and psychological needs.

It is so easy for many of us to have compassion for others, especially when they make mistakes. However, what happens when something goes wrong, or we are going through a challenging time? How compassionately do other people react to us in our challenging times? Do they have the same amount of compassion as you have for them?

Moreover, one thing I have learned in my life is that we often give to others the most of what we need, the most of ourselves. We give the most to other people because it is an indirect and safe way to feel access to the emotional resource ourselves. We need other people and their experiences to fulfill our own needs.

However, it will not always be enough because it ultimately does not return to you. So, you will always feel some level of absence within that. Then, because of that absence, you end up giving more and more. It is because you become used to the pattern of feeling that you are receiving some element of that, but you want more.

You want more, so what do you do? You repeat the action that allowed you to access that emotional element. You become stuck in a pattern where you give, give, and give. Sounds familiar? You are connecting the dots by now because it is imperative, as these patterns might show up in your relationships.

What if you are giving too much? It usually has a direct correlation to your mother. You may give a lot because you saw your mother giving a lot. Now, when you also look at the biological connection of the ancestors and how you are interpreting mothers right now and showing up in your life as well, you realize mothers played a role of being very feminine, gentle, and compassionate.

The feminine role is the mother role. However, some of you might have had a very abrasive and masculine mother.

Maybe she had to take care of everything, which took that feminine role away. We can see how this relationship with your mother is showing up in your life by understanding how it affects your relationship with yourself and others.

If the mother was very masculine, you could go two ways. You might copy that and think this is how a woman or a man should be. It depends on how you relate to that. Or you might look for partners that will aggressively nurture you because that is what your association is with nurturing.

This same would be right for the father's side as well. So if your dad was very masculine and abrasive, you might be looking for very abrasive or aggressive leadership. Or you might look for partners who are the opposite.

It is essential to observe how it plays out in your life. If your mother was very feminine, you might also look for it in a partner. It also depends on the wounds that you have with your mom. However, it is not necessarily about what your mom was doing wrong. It is more about looking at how you reacted to your mother. How did she emotionally influence you? How did it affect you?

Now, when we look at the connection with your mother, I would love to ask you, "What did you need from your mother? What did you emotionally need?" It is because our parents eventually show up in their absolute best possible way, even in an abusive way.

Answer: _____

Another important thing I have noticed and learned in my life is that when you become a parent and feel incompetent and do not know what to do with your role as a parent, you go back to your default (the way you were raised). It is because of how you were raised.

So, it highlights another critical question. How did your mother raise you? What was your dynamic with her? How did your dad raise you? How was your dynamic with your father?

I would also like you to think, "What did you emotionally need from your parents?" Whatever that unmet emotional need is, I am sure there is an intense part of you that feels hurt, wounded, and neglected. It now also begs the question, "Was your mother emotionally capable of showing up that way?" Here is the thing. There might have been moments and glimpses where she could show up in a certain way.

Maybe she was not able to hold that distressing situation for long periods. Maybe there were little bursts of moments where she could not be the mother you needed her to be. Maybe she had her emotional trauma, emotional blocks, and wounds. Maybe she was triggered by just life itself or her dynamic with your father and other people. Maybe she did not always have the tools or the capacity to move back into being the mother role you needed. You may have misinterpreted her inability to return to that role as a sign that you do not deserve her love.

It was never an indication of what you were worthy of. It reflects what your mother was emotionally and psychologically capable of. Moreover, her inability to show up in a certain way was never your fault. It never really had anything to do with you. It was just her weakness and inability to step up for you. Understanding is essential because it helps you heal by putting off that enormous emotional burden you might have been carrying. I am talking about that emotional burden where you always felt like you were never good enough; you are unworthy or do not deserve to be acknowledged, listened to, or attended to.

Another essential part that I want to clarify here for you is understanding and allowing yourself to accept your mother the way she is, which does not mean you are making excuses. It does not mean that you are accepting any injustice you faced in the past; there are no excuses for that. However, the part that you are accepting and realizing is that maybe there was a part of your mother that could not show up in the way you wanted. So, accept her with all her failures, flaws, and inabilities because you cannot change her.

We all show up every day and do our best with the help of awareness, mindfulness, emotional resources, and personal development tools that we can access.

Another vital part I invite you to consider is emotional attachment. Your emotional attachment to the need to have your mother act a certain way is holding you back from ultimately healing. It is holding you back from stepping into your power to find your self-worth. So, what is happening is that you constantly feel you are not worthy or good enough. The more your mother cannot act in a certain way for you, the more you feel you are not worthy or good enough. You feel you are not worthy of having your needs fulfilled; you are not worthy of being acknowledged;

you are not worthy of being heard. So, your self-esteem and self-worth diminish, and why it drops is because of your emotional need from your mother that she cannot fulfill.

Perhaps your emotional need made her feel uncomfortable or inadequate as a mother. She might need to learn what was expected of her and how to act in a certain way. Maybe she was trying to do her best, but her values and how she showed up were different. Maybe you misunderstood that she was not giving you what you wanted while she was giving it; however, different.

For example, two people feel that they are doing their best. They want their needs met, and there is an absolute mismatch, but the intention behind both experiences is well-intended. However, these intentions are also not aligned; they are not connecting.

That disconnection feels like a rejection. I invite you to observe that. You should consciously focus on it because it will trigger your mindfulness and cognitive awareness of what you felt happened versus what might have happened. Consciously think about the following questions as well.

Here I have a few questions for you.

What did you need from your mother?

_____

How are you trying to obtain this from your relationships?

_____

What steps can you take to release your partner from fulfilling a role they are not responsible for?

_____

There is tremendous power in these answers. These answers will assist you in building healthy relationships that are not based on old wounds but bringing forward your greatest self.

About the Author

Evette Rose is an Author, Life Coach, Metaphysical Anatomy Technique (M.A.T) development company and founder of several books. Evette was born in South Africa and grew up in Namibia, West Africa. She then moved to Australia, lived in Vanuatu and Bali. She is best known for her work in helping people to resolve trauma from their past and freeing them to live successful and fulfilling lives. Evette's work is drawn from her own personal experience of moving from a difficult past into a well-balanced life and career. Evette's philosophy is that we, as a human race, are not destined to live our lives in pain because of past trauma or abuse. We often suppress our ability to complete or heal trauma naturally. In today's society, we often suppress our pain in order to keep up with life and avoid being left behind. Fortunately, through gentle therapy, this natural internal healing instinct can be restored. Writing her books has helped Evette reach out to other people who need love, support, and someone to relate to. She shares her experiences with the world, hoping it will help people heal and provide encouragement and reassurance when they need it most. Evette now travels the world teaching personal development seminars and continues her research journey. She has been to well over 40 countries and worked with thousands of people!

References
1. Walter H, Gutierrez K, Ramskogler K, Hertling I, Dvorak A, Lesch OM. Gender-specific differences in alcoholism: Implications for treatment. *Arch Womens Ment Health*. 2003;6:253–8. [PubMed] [Google Scholar]
2. Blum LN, Nielsen NH, Riggs JA. Alcoholism and alcohol abuse among women: Report of the Council on Scientific Affairs. American Medical Association. *J Womens Health*. 1998;7:861–71. [PubMed] [Google Scholar]
3. Gilpin NW, Koob GF. Neurobiology of alcohol dependence: Focus on motivational mechanisms. *Alcohol Res Health*. 2008;31:185–95. [PMC free article] [PubMed] [Google Scholar]
4. Ji D, Gilpin NW, Richardson HN, Rivier CL, Koob GF. Effects of naltrexone, duloxetine, and a corticotropin-releasing factor type 1 receptor antagonist on binge-like alcohol drinking in rats. *Behav Pharmacol*. 2008;19:1–12. [PMC free article][PubMed] [Google Scholar]
5. Koob GF. Alcoholism: Allostasis and beyond. *Alcohol Clin Exp Res*. 2003;27:232–43. [PubMed] [Google Scholar]
6. Valdez GR, Roberts AJ, Chan K, Davis H, Brennan M, Zorrilla EP, et al. Increased ethanol self-administration and anxiety-like behavior during acute ethanol withdrawal and protracted abstinence: Regulation by corticotropin-releasing factor. *Alcohol Clin Exp Res*. 2002;26:1494–501. [PubMed] [Google Scholar]
7. Hodge CW, Samson HH, Chappelle AM. Alcohol self-administration: Further examination of the role of dopamine receptors in the nucleus accumbens. *Alcohol Clin Exp Res*. 1997;21:1083–91. [PubMed] [Google Scholar]
8. Rassnick S, Pulvirenti L, Koob GF. Oral ethanol self-administration in rats is reduced by the administration of dopamine and glutamate receptor antagonists into the nucleus accumbens. *Psychopharmacology (Berl)* 1992;109:92–8. [PubMed] [Google Scholar]
9. Weiss F, Lorang MT, Bloom FE, Koob GF. Oral alcohol self-administration stimulates dopamine release in the rat nucleus accumbens: Genetic and motivational determinants. *J Pharmacol Exp Ther*. 1993;267:250–8. [PubMed] [Google Scholar]
10. Rassnick S, Stinus L, Koob GF. The effects of 6-hydroxydopamine lesions of the nucleus accumbens and the mesolimbic dopamine system on oral self-administration of ethanol in the rat. *Brain Res*. 1993;623:16–24. [PubMed] [Google Scholar]
11. Volkow ND, Wang GJ, Telang F, Fowler JS, Logan J, Jayne M, et al. Profound decreases in dopamine release in striatum in detoxified alcoholics: Possible orbitofrontal involvement. *J Neurosci*. 2007;27:12700–6. [PMC free article] [PubMed] [Google Scholar]

12. Virkkunen M, Linnoila M. Serotonin in early onset, male alcoholics with violent behaviour. *Ann Med.* 1990;22:327–31.[PubMed] [Google Scholar]

13. Johnson BA. Update on neuropharmacological treatments for alcoholism: Scientific basis and clinical findings. *Biochem Pharmacol.* 2008;75:34–56. [PMC free article] [PubMed] [Google Scholar]

14. Weiss F, Parsons LH, Schulteis G, Hyytiä P, Lorang MT, Bloom FE, et al. Ethanol self-administration restores withdrawal-associated deficiencies in accumbal dopamine and 5-hydroxytryptamine release in dependent rats. *J Neurosci.* 1996;16:3474–85. [PMC free article] [PubMed] [Google Scholar]

15. Koob GF. A role for GABA mechanisms in the motivational effects of alcohol. *Biochem Pharmacol.* 2004;68:1515–25.[PubMed] [Google Scholar]

16. Hyytiä P, Koob GF. GABAA receptor antagonism in the extended amygdala decreases ethanol self-administration in rats. *Eur J Pharmacol.* 1995;283:151–9. [PubMed] [Google Scholar]

17. Roberto M, Madamba SG, Moore SD, Tallent MK, Siggins GR. Ethanol increases GABAergic transmission at both pre- and postsynaptic sites in rat central amygdala neurons. *Proc Natl Acad Sci U S A.* 2003;100:2053–8. [PMC free article][PubMed] [Google Scholar]

18. Roberto M, Madamba SG, Stouffer DG, Parsons LH, Siggins GR. Increased GABA release in the central amygdala of ethanol-dependent rats. *J Neurosci.* 2004;24:10159–66. [PMC free article] [PubMed] [Google Scholar]

19. Harvey SC, Foster KL, McKay PF, Carroll MR, Seyoum R, Woods JE, 2nd, et al. The GABA (A) receptor alpha1 subtype in the ventral pallidum regulates alcohol-seeking behaviors. *J Neurosci.* 2002;22:3765–75. [PMC free article] [PubMed] [Google Scholar]

20. June HL, Foster KL, McKay PF, Seyoum R, Woods JE, Harvey SC, et al. The reinforcing properties of alcohol are mediated by GABA (A1) receptors in the ventral pallidum. *Neuropsychopharmacology.* 2003;28:2124–37. [PubMed] [Google Scholar]

21. Biggio G, Concas A, Follesa P, Sanna E, Serra M. Stress, ethanol, and neuroactive steroids. *Pharmacol Ther.* 2007;116:140–71. [PMC free article] [PubMed] [Google Scholar]

22. Lambert JJ, Belelli D, Harney SC, Peters JA, Frenguelli BG. Modulation of native and recombinant GABA (A) receptors by endogenous and synthetic neuroactive steroids. *Brain Res Brain Res Rev.* 2001;37:68–80. [PubMed] [Google Scholar]

23. VanDoren MJ, Matthews DB, Janis GC, Grobin AC, Devaud LL, Morrow AL. Neuroactive steroid 3alpha-hydroxy-5alpha-pregnan-20-one modulates electrophysiological and behavioral actions of ethanol. *J Neurosci.* 2000;20:1982–9. [PMC free article] [PubMed] [Google Scholar]

24. Sanna E, Talani G, Busonero F, Pisu MG, Purdy RH, Serra M, et al. Brain steroidogenesis mediates ethanol modulation of GABAA receptor activity in

rat hippocampus. *J Neurosci.* 2004;24:6521–30. [PMC free article] [PubMed] [Google Scholar]

25. Carboni S, Isola R, Gessa GL, Rossetti ZL. Ethanol prevents the glutamate release induced by N-methyl-D-aspartate in the rat striatum. *Neurosci Lett.* 1993;152:133–6. [PubMed] [Google Scholar]

26. Roberto M, Schweitzer P, Madamba SG, Stouffer DG, Parsons LH, Siggins GR. Acute and chronic ethanol alter glutamatergic transmission in rat central amygdala: An *in vitro* and *in vivo* analysis. *J Neurosci.* 2004;24:1594–603. [PMC free article] [PubMed] [Google Scholar]

27. Lovinger DM, White G, Weight FF. Ethanol inhibits NMDA-activated ion current in hippocampal neurons. *Science.* 1989;243:1721–4. [PubMed] [Google Scholar]

28. Blednov YA, Harris RA. Metabotropic glutamate receptor 5 (mGluR5) regulation of ethanol sedation, dependence and consumption: Relationship to acamprosate actions. *Int J Neuropsychopharmacol.* 2008;11:775–93. [PMC free article][PubMed] [Google Scholar]

29. Pulvirenti L, Diana M. Drug dependence as a disorder of neural plasticity: Focus on dopamine and glutamate. *Rev Neurosci.* 2001;12:141–58. [PubMed] [Google Scholar]

30. Littleton JM. Acamprosate in alcohol dependence: Implications of a unique mechanism of action. *J Addict Med.* 2007;1:115–25. [PubMed] [Google Scholar]

31. Spanagel R, Pendyala G, Abarca C, Zghoul T, Sanchis-Segura C, Magnone MC, et al. The clock gene Per2 influences the glutamatergic system and modulates alcohol consumption. *Nat Med.* 2005;11:35–42. [PubMed] [Google Scholar]

32. Prasad P, Ambekar A, Vaswani M. Dopamine D2 receptor polymorphisms and susceptibility to alcohol dependence in Indian males: A preliminary study. *BMC Med Genet.* 2010;11:24. [PMC free article] [PubMed] [Google Scholar]

33. Neville MJ, Johnstone EC, Walton RT. Identification and characterization of ANKK1: A novel kinase gene closely linked to DRD2 on chromosome band 11q23.1. *Hum Mutat.* 2004;23:540–5. [PubMed] [Google Scholar]

34. Usiello A, Baik JH, Rougé-Pont F, Picetti R, Dierich A, LeMeur M, et al. Distinct functions of the two isoforms of dopamine D2 receptors. *Nature.* 2000;408:199–203. [PubMed] [Google Scholar]

35. Connor JP, Young RM, Lawford BR, Ritchie TL, Noble EP. D (2) dopamine receptor (DRD2) polymorphism is associated with severity of alcohol dependence. *Eur Psychiatry.* 2002;17:17–23. [PubMed] [Google Scholar]

36. Esposito-Smythers C, Spirito A, Rizzo C, McGeary JE, Knopik VS. Associations of the DRD2 TaqIA polymorphism with impulsivity and substance use: Preliminary results from a clinical sample of

adolescents. *Pharmacol Biochem Behav.* 2009;93:306–12. [PMC free article] [PubMed] [Google Scholar]

37. Berggren U, Fahlke C, Berglund KJ, Wadell K, Zetterberg H, Blennow K, et al. Dopamine D2 receptor genotype is associated with increased mortality at a 10-year follow-up of alcohol-dependent individuals. *Alcohol Alcohol.* 2010;45:1–5.[PubMed] [Google Scholar]

38. Pinto E, Reggers J, Gorwood P, Boni C, Scantamburlo G, Pitchot W, et al. The TaqI A DRD2 polymorphism in type II alcohol dependence: A marker of age at onset or of a familial disease? *Alcohol.* 2009;43:271–5. [PubMed] [Google Scholar]

39. Shaikh KJ, Naveen D, Sherrin T, Murthy A, Thennarasu K, Anand A, et al. Polymorphisms at the DRD2 locus in early-onset alcohol dependence in the Indian population. *Addict Biol.* 2001;6:331–5. [PubMed] [Google Scholar]

40. Konishi T, Calvillo M, Leng AS, Lin KM, Wan YJ. Polymorphisms of the dopamine D2 receptor, serotonin transporter, and GABA (A) receptor beta (3) subunit genes and alcoholism in Mexican-Americans. *Alcohol.* 2004;32:45–52. [PubMed] [Google Scholar]

41. Konishi T, Luo HR, Calvillo M, Mayo MS, Lin KM, Wan YJ. ADH1B*1, ADH1C*2, DRD2 (-141C Ins), and 5-HTTLPR are associated with alcoholism in Mexican American men living in Los Angeles. *Alcohol Clin Exp Res.* 2004;28:1145–52.[PubMed] [Google Scholar]

42. Lucht M, Barnow S, Schroeder W, Grabe HJ, Rosskopf D, Brummer C, et al. Alcohol consumption is associated with an interaction between DRD2 exon 8 A/A genotype and self-directedness in males. *Neuropsychobiology.* 2007;56:24–31.[PubMed] [Google Scholar]

43. Noble EP. The D2 dopamine receptor gene: A review of association studies in alcoholism and phenotypes. *Alcohol.* 1998;16:33–45. [PubMed] [Google Scholar]

44. Samochowiec J, Kucharska-Mazur J, Grzywacz A, Jabłoński M, Rommelspacher H, Samochowiec A, et al. Family-based and case-control study of DRD2, DAT, 5HTT, COMT genes polymorphisms in alcohol dependence. *Neurosci Lett.* 2006;410:1–5. [PubMed] [Google Scholar]

45. Florez G, Saiz P, Garcia-Portilla P, Alvarez S, Nogueiras L, Morales B, et al. Association between the Stin2 VNTR polymorphism of the serotonin transporter gene and treatment outcome in alcohol-dependent patients. *Alcohol Alcohol.* 2008;43:516–22. [PubMed] [Google Scholar]

46. Wiesbeck GA, Dürsteler-MacFarland KM, Wurst FM, Walter M, Petitjean S, Müller S, et al. No association of dopamine receptor sensitivity *in vivo* with genetic predisposition for alcoholism and DRD2/DRD3 gene polymorphisms in alcohol dependence. *Addict Biol.* 2006;11:72–5. [PubMed] [Google Scholar]

47. Johann M, Putzhammer A, Eichhammer P, Wodarz N. Association of the -141C Del variant of the dopamine D2 receptor (DRD2) with positive family

history and suicidality in German alcoholics. *Am J Med Genet B Neuropsychiatr Genet.* 2005;132B:46–9. [PubMed] [Google Scholar]

48. Crockett MJ, Clark L, Tabibnia G, Lieberman MD, Robbins TW. Serotonin modulates behavioral reactions to unfairness. *Science.* 2008;320:1739. [PMC free article] [PubMed] [Google Scholar]

49. Benmansour S, Cecchi M, Morilak DA, Gerhardt GA, Javors MA, Gould GG, et al. Effects of chronic antidepressant treatments on serotonin transporter function, density, and mRNA level. *J Neurosci.* 1999;19:10494–501. [PMC free article][PubMed] [Google Scholar]

50. Lesch KP, Bengel D, Heils A, Sabol SZ, Greenberg BD, Petri S, et al. Association of anxiety-related traits with a polymorphism in the serotonin transporter gene regulatory region. *Science.* 1996;274:1527–31. [PubMed] [Google Scholar]

51. Caspi A, Sugden K, Moffitt TE, Taylor A, Craig IW, Harrington H, et al. Influence of life stress on depression: Moderation by a polymorphism in the 5-HTT gene. *Science.* 2003;301:386–9. [PubMed] [Google Scholar]

52. Levinson DF. The genetics of depression: A review. *Biol Psychiatry.* 2006;60:84–92. [PubMed] [Google Scholar]

53. Heils A, Teufel A, Petri S, Stöber G, Riederer P, Bengel D, et al. Allelic variation of human serotonin transporter gene expression. *J Neurochem.* 1996;66:2621–4. [PubMed] [Google Scholar]

54. Wang XJ, Zhong SR, Bao JJ, Dou SJ, Wu WY, Jing Q. Association of polymorphism in the serotonin transporter gene promote with the susceptibility to alcohol dependence in Yunnan Han Population. *Yi Chuan.* 2011;33:48–53. [PubMed] [Google Scholar]

55. Ho PS, Shih MC, Ma KH, Huang WS, Ho KK, Yen CH, et al. Availability of the serotonin transporter in patients with alcohol dependence. *World J Biol Psychiatry.* 2011;12:134–42. [PubMed] [Google Scholar]

56. Merenäkk L, Mäestu J, Nordquist N, Parik J, Oreland L, Loit HM, et al. Effects of the serotonin transporter (5-HTTLPR) and α2A-adrenoceptor (C-1291G) genotypes on substance use in children and adolescents: A longitudinal study. *Psychopharmacology (Berl)* 2011;215:13–22. [PubMed] [Google Scholar]

57. Enoch MA, Gorodetsky E, Hodgkinson C, Roy A, Goldman D. Functional genetic variants that increase synaptic serotonin and 5-HT3 receptor sensitivity predict alcohol and drug dependence. *Mol Psychiatry.* 2011;16:1139–46. [PMC free article][PubMed] [Google Scholar]

58. Armeli S, Conner TS, Covault J, Tennen H, Kranzler HR. A serotonin transporter gene polymorphism (5-HTTLPR), drinking-to-cope motivation, and negative life events among college students. *J Stud Alcohol Drugs.* 2008;69:814–23. [PMC free article] [PubMed] [Google Scholar]

59. van der Zwaluw CS, Kuntsche E, Engels RC. Risky alcohol use in adolescence: The role of genetics (DRD2, SLC6A4) and coping motives. *Alcohol Clin Exp Res.* 2011;35:756–64. [PubMed] [Google Scholar]
60. Herman AI, Philbeck JW, Vasilopoulos NL, Depetrillo PB. Serotonin transporter promoter polymorphism and differences in alcohol consumption behaviour in a college student population. *Alcohol Alcohol.* 2003;38:446–9. [PubMed] [Google Scholar]
61. Saiz PA, Garcia-Portilla MP, Florez G, Arango C, Corcoran P, Morales B, et al. Differential role of serotonergic polymorphisms in alcohol and heroin dependence. *Prog Neuropsychopharmacol Biol Psychiatry.* 2009;33:695–700.[PubMed] [Google Scholar]
62. Dick DM, Plunkett J, Wetherill LF, Xuei X, Goate A, Hesselbrock V, et al. Association between GABRA1 and drinking behaviors in the collaborative study on the genetics of alcoholism sample. *Alcohol Clin Exp Res.* 2006;30:1101–10. [PubMed] [Google Scholar]
63. Park CS, Park SY, Lee CS, Sohn JW, Hahn GH, Kim BJ. Association between alcoholism and the genetic polymorphisms of the GABAA receptor genes on chromosome 5q33-34 in Korean population. *J Korean Med Sci.* 2006;21:533–8. [PMC free article] [PubMed] [Google Scholar]
64. Chang YT, Sun HS, Fann CS, Chang CJ, Liao ZH, Huang JL, et al. Association of the gamma-aminobutyric acid A receptor gene cluster with alcohol dependence in Taiwanese Han. *Mol Psychiatry.* 2002;7:828–9. [PubMed] [Google Scholar]
65. Dick DM, Edenberg HJ, Xuei X, Goate A, Hesselbrock V, Schuckit M, et al. No association of the GABAA receptor genes on chromosome 5 with alcoholism in the collaborative study on the genetics of alcoholism sample. *Am J Med Genet B Neuropsychiatr Genet.* 2005;132B:24–8. [PubMed] [Google Scholar]
66. Song J, Koller DL, Foroud T, Carr K, Zhao J, Rice J, et al. Association of GABA (A) receptors and alcohol dependence and the effects of genetic imprinting. *Am J Med Genet B Neuropsychiatr Genet.* 2003;117B:39–45. [PubMed] [Google Scholar]
67. Rolland B, Karila L, Guardia D, Cottencin O. Pharmaceutical approaches of binge drinking. *Curr Pharm Des.* 2011;17:1333–42. [PubMed] [Google Scholar]
68. Domart MC, Benyamina A, Lemoine A, Bourgain C, Blecha L, Debuire B, et al. Association between a polymorphism in the promoter of a glutamate receptor subunit gene (GRIN2A) and alcoholism. *Addict Biol.* 2012;17:783–5. [PubMed] [Google Scholar]
https://www.theguardian.com/lifeandstyle/2019/mar/02/abuse-prevention-how-to-turn-off-the-gaslighters?fbclid=IwAR0gZWGJKcmk0QaSI_sOEA7vLzlSlzjahVtyzIsPByT0uicdKOQGLy_0SM8

https://themindfool.com/narcissist/

https://blog.sivanaspirit.com/hh-cellular-level-every-single-human-depends-on-positivity-to-survive/

https://universallighthous.wixsite.com/loveandlight/post/scientists-prove-dna-can-be-reprogrammed-by-our-own-words

https://www.mentalhelp.net/anger/physiology/

https://www.betterhealth.vic.gov.au/health/healthyliving/anger-how-it-affects-people

Printed in Great Britain
by Amazon

46099366R00145